Wonders of the Natural Mind

The Essence of Dzogchen in the Native Bon Tradition of Tibet

Wonders of the Natural Mind

The Essence of Dzogchen in the
Native Bon Tradition of Tibet

by
Tenzin Wangyal Rinpoche

Foreword by
H. H. the Dalai Lama

edited by
Andrew Lukianowicz

Snow Lion Publications
Ithaca, NY USA

Snow Lion Publications
605 West State Street
P.O. Box 6483
Ithaca, NY 14851
607-273-8519
www.snowlionpub.com

Photographs on pages 120, 127, and 181 by Charles Stein © 1993
Charles Stein. Photograph on page 20 by Susan Rothschild © 1993
Susan Rothschild. Drawings on pages 25-30 by Paola Minelli. © 1993
Paola Minelli. Photograph on page 8 by Alison Wright © Alison
Wright. All other photographs courtesy of the author.

ISBN-13 978-1-55939-142-9

Printed in Canada on acid-free recycled paper.

Library of Congress Cataloging-in-Publication Data

Wangyal, Tenzin
    Wonders of the natural mind : the essence of Dzogchen in the native Bon
tradition of Tibet / Tenzin Wangyal ; foreword by H. H. Dalai Lama ; edited
by Andrew Lukianowicz.
    p. cm.
    ISBN 1-55939-142-1
    1. Rdzogs-chen (Bonpo) 2. Bonpo (Sect) — Doctrines. 3. Meditation — Bonpo
(Sect) 4. Wangyal, Tenzin. 5. Bonpo Lamas — China — Tibet — Biography. I.
Lukianowicz, Andrew. II. Title.

    BQ7982.3.W35 2000
    299'.54--dc21   00-036576

Contents

Tenzin Wangyal Rinpoche

His Holiness the Dalai Lama

Foreword

Bon is Tibet's oldest spiritual tradition and, as the indigenous source of Tibetan culture, played a significant role in shaping Tibet's unique identity. Consequently, I have often stressed the importance of preserving this tradition. This book, *Wonders of the Natural Mind*, containing teachings given abroad by the young Bonpo Geshe, Tenzin Wangyal, is ample evidence that this is being done.

With the Chinese invasion of our homeland, like Tibet's other spiritual traditions, Bon also faced irreparable losses. However, due to the efforts of the Bonpo community in exile, a number of Bon monasteries have been reestablished in India and Nepal. Visiting Tashi Menri Ling Monastery at Dolanji in the hills near Solan, Himachal Pradesh, India, I have been encouraged to see that it has become a major centre of Bonpo learning.

This book will be of great help to readers wishing to find a clear explanation of the Bon tradition, especially with regard to its presentation of the teachings of Dzogchen, and I congratulate all those who contributed to bringing it out.

— His Holiness the Dalai Lama

His Holiness Lungtog Tenpai Nyima

གཡུང་དྲུང་བོན་འཛིན་སློང་ལུ་ཚོགས།

**YUNG-DRUNG BON
MONASTIC CENTRE**

Tel. No. 334 Ochghat

Post Office Ochghat,
Via Solan, 173 223,
Himachal Pradesh
INDIA.

In the west recently a number of books have appeared on the subject of Dzog Chen. This is the first book to describe the Bon-Po point of view of these high teachings. This pleases me greatly. They are derived from the Zhang Zhung Nyan Gyud, which is the most essential within the Bon-Po Dzog Chen.

Lama Tenzin Wangyal Rinpoche has been trained in this lineage since he was fourteen by the Venerable Lopan Sanje Tenzin and the Venerable Lopan Tenzin Namdak. From the early days on he has shown a special gift when it comes to these meditations.

The book is written in clear and consise English. This is particuarly important as the teachings are very elaborate and at times hard to understand. The simple language used clarifies tremendously. The authentic descriptions of Dzog Chen give the serious student ample mns material to practice Dzog Chen.

This book doesnt include stories it explains the quinticential aspects of Dzog Chen. In other words it gets right to the point. Especially the chapters such as the ones on Contemplation and Integration. I highly recommend this book to any serious student of these high teachings.

Lungtok Tenpai Nyima.

This book is dedicated to my mother

Preface

Western readers may be surprised to find a Tibetan tradition with a practice and doctrine essentially the same as the spiritual teachings of the four well-known Tibetan Buddhist schools but which does not call itself "Buddhist" and does not trace its lineage back to the Indian Prince, Shakyamuni. But Bon is just such a tradition. It is not "Buddhist" if we define Buddhism as a religion stemming from that Enlightened Indian Prince, but it does nevertheless derive from a Buddha — Shenrab Miwoche — who, according to Bon tradition, lived and taught in Central Asia 17,000 years ago! This book will not be concerned with arguments over the historical claims of this tradition. I do, however, assume the authenticity of its spiritual teaching.

In particular, this book involves a presentation of the Dzogchen tradition. Dzogchen has begun to be familiar to Westerners through the teachings of the Nyingmapa school, His Holiness the Dalai Lama, and other Tibetan teachers residing and teaching in Western countries. Dzogchen is in fact a complete teaching in itself, with its own View, Meditation, and Practices, and it is essentially the same whatever the context of its presentation. I have given in this work the Dzogchen teachings as they are developed in the Bon tradition, and have addressed the text primarily to current and prospective Dzogchen practitioners. I have therefore emphasized a direct presentation of the actual content of the teachings rather than a treatment of historical or technical matters, and I have tried to capture the essence of the main points of Dzogchen in contemporary English that does not rely too heavily on the technical vocabulary and phraseology of Tibetan texts. The use of some Tibetan terms, of course, is unavoidable, but I have tried to provide colloquial translations and adequate explanations.

Presenting Dzogchen in this direct way should be helpful to beginners and advanced practitioners alike. For beginners it should be useful because it does not depend on detailed knowledge of the tradition and vocabulary, but for advanced practitioners it should be useful too. Persons familiar with many texts and traditions may find it of value to have a succinct summary of the essential points of Dzogchen giving a synoptic overview of the tradition and its structure. Such a direct approach is actually very much in the spirit of Dzogchen itself. Though Dzogchen can be elaborated in manifold ways, it always retains the essential structure of its original points throughout.

I have developed this text from my experiences teaching Dzogchen in the West over the last five years and have chosen my particular emphasis in accordance with what it seems to me contemporary students need to hear about. Yet I have remained, I hope, at every point rigorously faithful to the "Dzogchen View." The teachings are not a system of abstract thought that exist apart from actual practitioners, though the principles and the view of Dzogchen remain constant and pure.

This text is composed from my recent oral teaching, based on the *Zhang Zhung Nyan Gyud*, but I have not attempted to follow precisely the structure of these texts.

Let me reiterate that this is a book primarily for persons interested in exploring Dzogchen as a spiritual path. Of the three aspects of any Buddhist teaching — View, Meditation, and Activity — in Dzogchen the View is considered most important. Since a text like the present one is concerned primarily with communicating the View, it is surely the case that an important part of the teaching can be received by the sensitive reader from studying the text alone. Yet, at the same time, confirmation and development of one's understanding by an authentic Dzogchen Master is essential for progress on the path.

I would like to thank my teachers, both Bon and Buddhist, from whom I have received the transmission of the knowledge contained in this book, and my editor, Andrew Lukianowicz. I would also like to thank Anne Klein and Charles Stein for their help in preparing the manuscript, Harvey Aronson for reading it, Anthony Curtis for preparing the glossary, George and Susan Quasha for their hospitality while preparing the work and for their collaboration; and Namkhai Norbu Rinpoche for all the help that he gave me during my stay in the West, particularly in Italy.

Lopon Sangye Tenzin Rinpoche

1

My Life and Experiences of the Teaching

My Parents and Early Childhood

When the Chinese overran Tibet in 1959, both my parents, who came from different parts of Tibet, fled through Nepal to India, where they met and married. My father was a Nyingmapa "Dunglu Lama" (of a lineage that is transmitted through family) and his name was Shampa Tentar. My mother's name was Yeshe Lhamo; she was a Bonpo and came from an important family in the Bon area of Hor. I am their only son and was born in Amritsar in northwest India. I spent my early years in the Tibetan Treling Kasang kindergarten in Simla in north India. When it closed, all the children were sent to different schools, and I went to a Christian school, which I attended until I was ten years old.

After my father died, my mother remarried and my stepfather was a Bon Lama. He and my mother decided I should not stay on in the Christian school. First I received some education from the Kagyupas, from whom I received the name Jigme Dorje; then my parents sent me to Dolanji in north India, where there is a Tibetan Bon village. Coming to live in a Tibetan community was a completely new experience for me.

Life at Dolanji

After one week I became a novice monk in the monastery. Because my stepfather was an influential Lama, I had two personal tutors. One, Lungkhar Gelong, taught me reading and writing and basic education, while the other taught me "worldly knowledge." He also took care of my clothes, cooked my food, and so forth. He was one of the respected elder monks and his name was Gen Singtruk.

I spent a couple of years with them living in the same house, and at that time I started to read the ritual texts, to write different Tibetan scripts, and to learn the prayers and invocations of the monastic practices. In those days my teacher Lungkhar Gelong used to study logic and philosophy together with a small group of people under Geshe Yungdrung Langyel. He was a "Geshe Lharampa" (the highest level of Geshe) in both the Bon and Gelugpa orders. Later Geshe Yungdrung Langyel was my main master in philosophy when I studied for my geshe degree.

The years with these two teachers were some of the hardest periods in my education, because I never had time to play with friends of my own age. All my time was spent in intensive study, and I was even happy when I could cook and clean the house because it was a break from studying. I saw that other young boys studied in a group, and my situation seemed much harder.

Receiving the Zhang Zhung Nyan Gyud Teachings

One of the elder monks at Dolanji asked the master Lopon Sangye Tenzin Rinpoche to give the *Zhang Zhung Nyan Gyud* teachings of Bon Dzogchen, and, when he agreed, my stepfather went to ask him if I could also receive these teachings. He gave his consent, saying that at the same time I should also start doing the *ngondro* (preliminary practices), *powa*, and *zhiné* meditation.

In order to be admitted to the teachings, before starting we were asked to recount our dreams to the master. These dreams served as signs, and as some practitioners did not dream, which was a bad sign, the master waited until everybody had dreams. According to the various dreams, he advised practices for purification, to remove obstacles, and to have contact with the Guardians in order to get their permission to receive the teachings. In my dream I was a bus ticket inspector, checking tickets that were like white *A*'s printed at the center of pieces of cloth or paper of five colors like five-colored *tiglés*. The master said this was an auspicious sign. A group of us, including Lopon Tenzin Namdak Rinpoche, started to receive the *Zhang Zhung Nyan Gyud* teachings. The group consisted of about fifteen monks and one layman, and all were over forty years old. I was the only young boy with all these adults.

After finishing the nine cycles of *ngondro*, I practiced *powa* with two other persons. We practiced individually, and I used to do the *powa* practice by myself in the storeroom of Lopon Tenzin Namdak's house. (The *powa* involves the transference of the consciousness principle in the form of a *tiglé* through a hole at the top of the head.) I also did my dark retreat in the same room. Since I was not practicing intensively, it took me about a week to get the result, which consisted of the fontanelle's softening and eventually forming an actual opening. On a couple of mornings, I went to Lopon Sangye Tenzin before the other students arrived and he looked at the top of my head but saw that the fontanelle had not yet softened. My friends teased me, saying my head was like stone, and Lopon Sangye Tenzin suggested I do some group *powa* practice, with me at the center and the older monks around me. Next morning when Lopon looked, he was at last able to insert a blade of *kusha* grass, which must stand upright in the hole in the fontanelle to demonstrate that the practice has been successful. The blade of grass was about twelve inches long and remained upright for three days. Sometimes I forgot I had it in my head and felt a painful sensation when I pulled my robe over my head, yanking the blade of grass. Also, if I walked in the street when it was windy, I felt as if an electric current were being channelled into the center of my body through the grass.

After *powa* I did *zhiné* meditation on *A* with Lopon Sangye Tenzin for quite a long time, and through this meditation I received the direct introduction to Dzogchen.

Lopon Tenzin Namdak Rinpoche

The Dzogchen teachings lasted three years. The only interruptions were for *ganapujas* and personal retreats. In fact, these were very sacred *kanye* teachings (teachings about which the Guardians are very sensitive). Often, even though a master may have the Guardians' permission to give a teaching, if there are any *samaya* (commitment) breakages or if respect for the teachings is lacking, the master will receive indications about this in dreams from the Guardians manifesting their displeasure. When this happened, Lopon Sangye Tenzin would interrupt the teaching for one or two days so we could do the Zhang Zhung Meri *ganapuja* to purify our intentions.

Lopon Sangye Tenzin used to teach at his big retreat house in Dolanji village. Nearby I could see a group of about five monks studying logic and debating during the intermissions in the monastic rituals. I watched them excitedly. Not being able to participate with them, I was fascinated by all their gestures and movements. When I told them what I was learning about Dzogchen, they couldn't understand me, and when they told me what they were debating, I couldn't understand them. These were the people who became *geshes* at the same time as I did, just like the teacher who taught me reading and writing.

Lopon Sangye Tenzin was not only very knowledgeable about Dzogchen, he had studied for many years in Drepung Monastery of the Gelugpa order and had also studied under masters of the other Tibetan Buddhist schools. He was very strict and taught in a way that was very direct and clear, making things understandable without needing to use a lot of words. Often, just being in the group made it easy to understand the teachings.

After we finished this cycle of teachings, we discussed what we should do next. By then Lopon Sangye Tenzin was not in good physical health, so we students decided to ask to receive the *Zhang Zhung Nyan Gyud* again. As the traditional instructions require, Lopon started again with the biographies of the lineage masters (which instruct by explaining the meaning and results of practice in masters' lives); then, as he couldn't continue, he said we should stop at that point, adding that it was a good sign that we had started and that now we should continue to receive the teachings from Lopon Tenzin Namdak. He told Lopon Tenzin Namdak that he should take over this great responsibility and told him very precisely that he should consider each aspect of the teaching, such as drawing the mandalas, etc., as equally important. Lopon Sangye Tenzin died a few months later, in 1977.

Life with Lopon Tenzin Namdak

I remember seeing Lopon Tenzin Namdak when he first arrived from Delhi. I went to greet him with a number of people, and I immediately felt a close connection with him. After some time he called me and told me that since one of his close disciples, Sherab Tsultrim, was ill and needed help, I should come and stay in his house to help him. Then one morning Lopon Tenzin Namdak called me and told me about a dream he had had. In the form of a black man, the deity Midu Gyampa Trangpo had come into his room, opened a partition curtain and, pointing at me, had told him, "You should take care of this young boy; he will be of future benefit." Lopon said this was an important dream and added that, as this deity was connected with Walse Ngampa, one of the five main Bon tantric deities, and as I was connected with these two deities, I should do the practices of these deities more assiduously.

When I lived in his house, Lopon Tenzin Namdak looked after me like a son; we slept in the same room, he cooked for me, and even sewed my clothes. At first I was the only person living there, then an old monk called Abo Tashi Tsering came to live with us and cook for us; eventually three other young boys came to live with us, and Lopon often jokingly referred to us as his "four sons without a mother." One of these boys was a fellow student at the Dialectic School, and we became close friends. He is Geshe Nyima Wangyal, who accompanied Lopon to the West in 1991.

When I first went to live with Tenzin Namdak he was already a *lopon*. He went to Lopon Sangye Tenzin's teachings because he wanted to refresh and improve his understanding of Dzogchen. We used to go together to receive the teachings and initiations. While I received the formal Dzogchen teachings of the *Zhang Zhung Nyan Gyud* from my first (in time) master, Lopon Sangye Tenzin, most of my personal growth came about in the period I spent with my second master, Lopon Tenzin Namdak.

From my early adolescence until I was a young man, my whole life took place in the presence of the Lopon. He was my father, mother, friend, teacher, and caretaker. It was an extraordinary and beautiful way to grow up, physically, emotionally, and spiritually. Apart from formal class sessions, every moment of being with him was Teaching.

It was while I was living with Lopon Tenzin Namdak that I met Namkhai Norbu Rinpoche, when he came to receive the initiation of Zhang Zhung Meri from the Lopon while travelling in India with a group of Italians who had come to make a film about Tibetan medicine. The initiation of this deity is necessary in order to study and practice the *Zhang Zhung Nyan Gyud* teachings. I was attracted by Norbu Rinpoche's general openness, his efforts to present the practice of Dzogchen in the West, and particularly his freedom from cultural bias against the Bon religion.

The Dialectics School

Lopon Sangye Tenzin had asked that after his death the money he left be spent to found a dialectics school leading to a *geshe* degree (equivalent to a Ph.D. in philosophy and metaphysical studies from a Western University). As soon as the school was founded, Lopon Tenzin Namdak was the first master to teach there, together with Lharampa Geshe Yungdrung Langyel, who taught philosophy and logic. I was among the first students, twelve in number, and we followed a very precise program of study of dialectics, philosophy, logic, poetry (I won top marks in a poetry competition), grammar, Tibetan astrology, and medicine. There was also a course in debating, which fascinated me very much, so much so that I became very skilled in debate.

In this school I was elected president among the six student representatives (there were also a vice-president, a secretary, vice-secretary, treasurer, and a *gekhod*, who was responsible for discipline). We met every ten days and held general meetings with the other students once a month. We became responsible for the administration of the school, planning courses and timetables; the monastery was responsible for providing two meals and tea every day, while the masters were responsible for the teaching. As president, I brought in some innovations, such as a course in creative writing and debates between classes.

The schedule at the dialectics school was very intense. We never had a fixed day off; we always had to attend six days in a row of classes and six evenings of debates; on the sixth night there was debating until three o'clock in the morning. This was followed by a holiday; but if a day of special practice interrupted the six days, then we lost the day of holiday. Every day we attended classes for eleven hours, with very short breaks. In the morning, Lopon Tenzin Namdak would teach from eight until twelve, and after lunch he would dedicate half an hour to giving transmissions from the *Zhang Zhung Nyan Gyud*, so that in nine years he was able to complete the transmission of the entire teachings. In the afternoon, he taught until around four or five, when he would retire to his room to meditate in the dark while we continued with our evening debating session. As soon as I finished, I would run home and switch on the light in his room, and he would immediately cover his eyes with his arms. Then he would teach me and Abo Tashi Tsering, or we three would practice together, or sometimes simply sit and talk.

Sometimes after school I would go to visit my mother, who lived nearby in Dolanji. To get there, I had to walk along a road that was supposedly haunted by demons. Lopon Tenzin Namdak would stand outside his house and talk to me continuously as I walked down the road, so I would not be afraid. When I could no longer hear his voice, I would run the rest of the way down to my mother's house in the village. As I did not sleep at her house, when I left, my mother would talk to me as I walked up the hill. As soon as I could no longer hear her voice, I would run the rest of the way back to Lopon's house.

In the morning Lopon would wake me up early (although sometimes I woke up before him) to repeat the texts I had memorized the previous evening and to write poems.

After a few years, the number of students at the dialectics school increased to over sixty and two teachers were no longer sufficient, so I started to teach. One of my first students was the current temporary Lopon at Dolanji, Yangal Tsewang, who is descended from a famous family of *jalupas*.

My Dark Retreat

Before he died Lopon Sangye Tenzin did something quite special. One day he called me and told me he had done some practice and written the names of some deities on pieces of paper and thrown them onto his altar. He asked me to pick up one of the pieces of

Thogal symbols

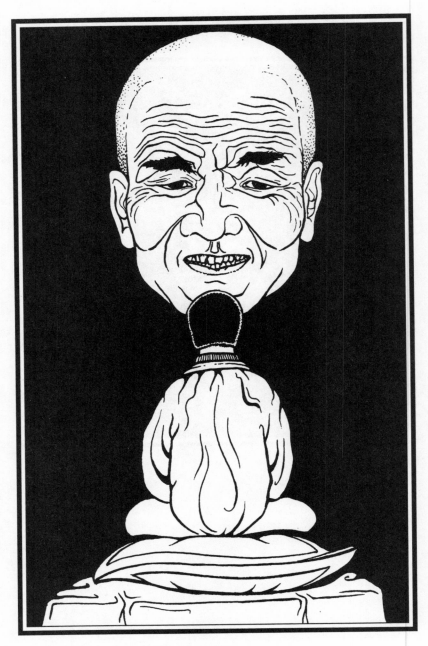

"I saw the huge bodyless head of Tashi Tsering...."

"... a man with his hair in a topknot like a mahasiddha..."

"I found myself in a big valley.... The wind was blowing through the trees and there was a long winding path along which five people were walking towards me."

" ... a plate of food with potatoes, tomatoes, and beans appeared and then transformed ..."

"Very clearly I could see fish swimming around in the limpid water."

paper; the name on the paper was the deity I was to practice. The deity I chose was Sherab Gyammo, a kind of Tara who is especially effective for developing the intellectual faculties. He also told me to do a dark retreat. I was very happy. Two years later, I asked for permission from Lopon Tenzin Namdak and my mother to do a dark retreat. They agreed, although my mother said she was worried because it was very unusual for such a young person to do a dark retreat. Some people in the monastery, who were probably envious, even said that I would probably go mad. Anyway, I arranged to do it in Lopon Tenzin Namdak's storeroom, which had been converted into a toilet for visiting guests. It was very small, around two by four meters, with cement walls, so the air circulation was very bad. My mother brought me food three times every day. During the dark retreat, I never spoke to her. Lopon and my mother became worried because I was not eating much at lunch or dinner during the retreat, perhaps because of the bad air, and thought that perhaps I should come out of the retreat early, but I completed the full forty-nine days.

Every day Lopon would come and sit outside the retreat hut and talk with me for half an hour. It was very important for me to be close to the master during this time. I could not remember all the teachings in advance, and as I had to change practices and visualizations every week, he would instruct me on these as appropriate. My mind was very void, empty, and without concepts during the times of practice; my experience was that it was good not to receive external information such as news. News creates a disturbance, giving rise to whole successions of thoughts that distract the mind from the practice. It was better to concentrate entirely on remaining present and developing clarity of mind. It was also very pleasant to think about the constructive way in which I was passing my time.

My dark retreat was very successful and brought about a great change in my personality. During the first few days it was not easy for me as a young boy with a lot of dynamic energy to stay confined and still in such a small, dark room. The first day I slept quite a lot; but already the second day was much better, and every day there was an improvement in my experience of the practice and my capacity to remain in the dark. It was a great experience in terms of being in contact with myself. Losing touch with influential external stimuli, such as eye sense-consciousness objects, became a way of totally entering into myself. I had heard stories and jokes about the problems people encountered while doing dark retreat, in which practitioners had visions they were sure were real, but I understood the way these could arise. In everyday life external appearances deflect us from our thoughts, but in the dark retreat there are no diversions of this kind, so that it becomes much easier to be disturbed, even to the point of madness, by our own mind-created visions. In the dark retreat, there is a situation of "sensory deprivation," so that when thoughts or visions arise in the absence of external reality-testing devices, we take them to be true and follow them, basing entire chains of thoughts on them. In this case it is very easy to become "submerged" in our own mind-created fantasies, entirely convinced of their "reality."

After the first week, my subjective sensation of time changed, so that seven days felt like two. In this way the last six weeks of the forty-nine day retreat felt like twelve days. Starting from the second week, I started to have many visions of rays of light, flashes of *tiglés*, rainbows, and different symbols. After the second week, the first forms resembling concrete reality started to appear.

The first of these visions came during the second morning session of the second week. While I was in the state of contemplation, I saw the huge, bodiless head of Abo Tashi Tsering before me in space. The head was enormous. The first few seconds I was afraid, and then I resumed my practice. The head remained in front of me for over half an hour; the vision was as clear as that of normal everyday external reality, and at times even clearer.

Gradually I had more experiences. For example, I saw a man with his hair in a topknot like a *mahasiddha*. The feeling was very strong and positive and empowering. Perhaps the most impressive vision was one that was accompanied by a lot of movement. Not all visions have movement; some are like watching a film; in some, you can find yourself inside the vision; in some, the vision is above you in space, or at the same level, or below. In this case I found myself in a big valley with hills covered with red flowers on both sides. The wind was blowing through beautiful trees, and there was a long, winding path along which five people were walking towards me. At the start they were so far away I could not distinguish their features, but after half an hour they had come so close I recognized them as Indians. Two were wearing Sikh turbans. They came up to me and then turned around and walked back, without saying anything.

Another time, I saw a long-lasting vision of a nude woman with long hair sitting straight ahead of me but turned away so that I couldn't see her face. When I saw these visions, they were not something appearing externally; they were the manifestations of my own mind in the form of light. Even when I closed my eyes I saw the visions in the same way but somehow sensed they were in different directions and locations.

Sometimes the visions changed from one form to another; for example, one vision of a plate of food with potatoes, tomatoes, and beans appeared and then transformed into a beautiful river with fish and stones. I could see fish swimming around in the limpid water very clearly. These were not the only visions I had but were simply the most remarkable ones.

Almost at the end of my retreat, my clarity increased greatly, so that I seemed to see what was going on outside the retreat hut. Once, with my mind's eye, I was aware of my mother bringing me food, "seeing" every step she took coming towards the house until she reached the door and knocked to tell me she had arrived. At the same time, I heard a knock on the door as my "real" mother told me she had come with my meal, so that the movements of my mother in my vision and the movements of my real mother had been synchronous.

There was no sound accompanying any of these visions, nor did I have any idea of trying to talk with the visions. Only after finishing the retreat did my intellectual mind start to think it would have been good to talk to them.

Through the retreat I purified many things in myself and developed my practice and clarity. One of my dreams after the retreat, which Lopon said was a sign of having achieved purification, was that I cut a vein in my left ankle with a knife and insects and blood came out. After my retreat, I became so calm and quiet that my mother said that all my sisters should do a dark retreat!

My Experiences in the West

Since my youth I have always felt a strong attraction for Western scientific methodology and the academic approach to religious studies, and after completing my studies in India, when I obtained my *geshe* degree, I wanted to continue my studies in the West. In Dolanji I met a number of Western scholars who were studying Bon, such as Professor Snellgrove, Professor Kvaerne, and Professor Blondeau. Per Kvaerne invited me to Norway to do a Ph.D. on the Bon Tantric deities at Oslo University, and Anton Geels, Professor of Psychology of Religion, invited me to Lund University in Sweden to work on research with his wife, who was translating the *Zhang Zhung Nyan Gyud*. At the same time Namkhai Norbu Rinpoche invited me to Merigar, the center of the Dzogchen Community in Italy. I waited two months to get an Italian visa and then finally with great difficulty managed to go to Italy. This was in January 1988. It was my second visit to Europe; I had already visited France, Belgium, and Germany in 1983 with the first tour of Bonpo Sacred Masked Dancers as group leader and performer.

When I arrived in Italy, I already had a number of Italian friends among the people who had visited Dolanji over the years. I stayed with Andrea dell'Angelo and Giacomella Orofino in Rome, and, since my residence permit was very short, after one week I went to extend it. At the same time I went with Enrico dell'Angelo to the IsMEO Institute in Rome where I was immediately offered a job, and since then I have worked there in the Library. Then I went up to Merigar: this was the first spiritual community I visited in the West.

Even though my intention in coming to the West had not been to teach but rather to study, when a small group of practitioners at a Dharma center in Milan, called Terra delle Dakini, invited me, I went to teach there. It was very strange for me to see that there was a fixed fee for the teachings, almost as if the teachings were being evaluated. Then I started to teach in numerous centers in Italy and elsewhere in Europe.

At first I felt uncomfortable teaching Dzogchen in the West, for a number of reasons: because the people were new and I did not know them, and because for me the Dzogchen teachings are the most important thing in my life. I didn't find the same respectful attitude at all in the West as when I received Dzogchen from my masters. Here in the West people seemed to consider it correct to talk about the teachings anywhere, and even sat in bars discussing teachings as in an ordinary conversation or in idle gossip. Also, I immediately noticed that what people were saying about the integration of Dzogchen with everyday life did not correspond with their normal behavior, which was lacking in compassion, mindfulness, skillfulness and awareness. Over time, I found that people would come for a weekend teaching and never return. There did not seem to be any personal connection, the kind of relationship that exists between master and student in a traditional context in Tibet or India, in which the master gives a method and the student practices it and then returns and tells the master about his experience. I didn't like this lack of continuous contact between master and student: here it seemed that going to hear teachings was just like attending an ordinary talk in a hall, so that sometimes it felt impersonal, and I felt almost like I was speaking on the radio.

For me transmitting Dzogchen is a responsibility. I want to make sure people understand what I am teaching, and sometimes I emphasize this aspect very strongly. But as time was often short, and because of the way of relating with people and the lack of feedback, it was often difficult to be sure about how people were receiving what I was teaching. People were often superficial rather than concrete and seemed to prefer to wait with blind faith for something mysterious to happen rather than to work in order to obtain direct experience. Some groups seemed very intellectual, some seemed very anti-intellectual. However, with the intention of helping others and mindful of what my master Lopon Sangye Tenzin had once said about the danger of the Dzogchen teaching dying out in the *kaliyuga*, I did my best to transmit the teachings.

On the positive side, I have found that it is easier to do group practice with lay people in the West than with Tibetan lay people in India or Tibet, where people are satisfied with initiations without necessarily knowing what they are receiving.

After a couple of months, on Easter in 1988, I led my first retreat at Merigar. On this occasion I wanted to give people the possibility to talk about their experiences. I was very pleased with how receptive newcomers were to the practices and teachings I was giving. After three months in Italy, I went to Scandinavia for about five months, where I worked on my thesis and also taught seminars in

Oslo, Copenhagen, and Stockholm. Then I went to England and gave teachings in London and Devon. I found that some Buddhists in the West had mistaken perceptions and misinformation about Bon and did not feel comfortable about coming to listen to teachings from a "Bon master." They sat far away at first but then would gradually come nearer as they recognized that I was giving Dzogchen teachings, without any labels.

I learned a lot during my first long visit to the West, and a couple of months after returning to India, I decided to come back to the West to work on my thesis while being employed at the IsMEO in Rome, to learn more about Western culture and psychology, and to work with the Dzogchen Community. While staying in Rome, people in the Dzogchen Community in Italy invited me to different cities to teach in Namkhai Norbu Rinpoche's absence (he was on a year's leave of absence from the university to undertake research in China), and I went as often as my other engagements and commitments allowed. I built up very good spiritual and friendly relationships with people in Italy. It was much more comfortable for me to see groups of people continuously, so there was a sense of process to the teachings I was giving them, creating more of a family feeling.

Further Reflections on the West

Another thing I wish to mention is that, among Western practitioners, the correct "view" or way of seeing the teachings sometimes seems to be lacking. I think that to preserve the teachings a special and specific spiritual view must be cultivated and maintained. This view exists in, and is part of, Tibetan culture, where it has helped to protect the teachings. A special self-preparation is needed in order to study the teachings and is even more necessary in the West. Obtaining this view is not impossible, and I have seen changes in many people who seriously and conscientiously follow the teachings.

I especially like teaching people who have received teachings from different masters, because in this way they have already perceived a different "taste" through the teachings and acquired a more general view. Also, as they already have some knowledge, I feel more satisfied when they appreciate what I am teaching; on the contrary, I have found that people who have received teachings from only one other master are more likely to compare my teaching with the other master's and make judgments.

Another thing I consider very important, and which I find is much misunderstood in the West, is the relationship between master and student. For example, if a student becomes a friend of the master, this aspect of the relationship must be kept separate from the spiritual or "dharmic" relationship; otherwise, if there is a breakdown in the friendship, this may lead to a breakdown in the dharmic relationship. Of course, this does not mean that master and student cannot be friends; however, in the East the dharmic relationship is always predominant over the worldly friendship. This creates a stronger bond than in the West. Perhaps it is because the sense of ego is stronger in the West that there is a greater need to "possess" the master as friend and constantly to have his positive evaluations.

There are some people who rebel against the strong Western educational emphasis on intellectual knowledge and so are attracted by masters who seem anti-intellectual, because in this way they can perpetuate their concepts or fantasies about "spirituality" rather than having to learn something new to develop their minds. But in fact the Dzogchen path also contains difficult concepts that require intellectual effort to grasp, as well as practices that allow the practitioner to observe and become aware of how specific practices affect and change his mind. On the other hand, a positive quality of many Western practitioners is that they want what they learn to have order. This leads to many precise questions about the teachings and the ways to do the practices, things often lacking among Tibetan practitioners.

Eventually there will be Western masters of Dzogchen and the other Tibetan spiritual traditions. This brings up the difficult problem of the degree to which the Tibetan cultural aspect of the teachings can be given up without the teachings losing their special quality. Any teaching taught in the West by a Tibetan master will undergo change by the very fact of being taught in a new and different cultural context, and the more successful a master is in communicating with the Western mind, the more he will have to change the teachings. But a good master will only change aspects

The author and His Holiness the Dalai Lama

that facilitate communication and will not change anything essential, as this would impair the purity of the teaching.

A problem that seems very difficult to avoid involves the tendency of spiritual schools either to want to preserve their traditions in a very closed way or to want to be very open and nonsectarian; but there is often the danger that this very nonsectarianism can become a source of self-justification and lead to as closed an attitude as that of the sectarians.

Another thing I have observed is that being a spiritual master can easily become an expression of the basic human passion of pride, so that the master becomes a leader like a military commander. Because of the spiritual connotations of being a master, this may seem less important to deal with than in the case of a commander, but I think that it is very important for masters to observe and work with this.

I would like to conclude by saying that, while it is necessary to keep the mantras in their original form, because their powerful effect lies in their sound, the prayers could be translated into English, because it is important to understand their meaning.

My First Visit to the U.S.A.

In January 1990, the year my mother passed away, I went to the United States for the first time, by invitation of the Dzogchen Community in Conway, Massachusetts. I travelled around the States for almost three months, visiting the Tibet Center in New York and other dharma centers and spiritual groups and also a number of universities, where I gave lectures totalling over 130 hours. While I was in the United States, Professor Anne Klein of Rice University in Houston invited me to give public teachings and lectures there. Although I had a very tight schedule, at the end of my trip I managed to arrange to go to Houston for a couple of days in April. I made a very good contact with Anne and we discussed future translation and study projects. Anne invited me back on behalf of Rice University, and I returned in August of the same year and stayed for two weeks. Together we worked on *Gal mdo*, a Bonpo Dzogchen text, and on texts dealing with the famous Bon deity Sridpa'i rGyalmo, the "Queen of Existence."

Plans for the Future

I left my work at IsMEO when I was awarded a Rockefeller Fellowship at Rice University for 1991-92. At Rice I have been lecturing, doing research, and attending the university classes on world religions. My stay in America and my work here has been very pleasant and comfortable thanks to the gracious support of Professor Anne Klein and her husband, Harvey Aronson. Even though I miss the beauty, the pace of life, and the friendliness of Italy, I have learned that it is very useful for me to be in America, where I am better able to continue my academic work.

I have many plans for the future. In 1992, my teacher, Lopon Tenzin Namdak, was in the United States to participate in the Kalachakra initiations in New York city. During his stay, he came to Houston and together we planned the program of the Ligmincha Institute and designed its logo. Encouraged by the dedicated and unrelenting efforts of my American friends and students, in particular, Anthony Curtis and Joan Kalyan Curtis, Victor and Virginia Torrico, John and Cindy Jackson, I am continuing with this plan. The Ligmincha Institute is named after the surname of the last kings of Zhang Zhung. It has been established in Virginia and will offer students a seven-year study program, including two years of Sutra, two of Tantra, and three of Dzogchen study, with the possibility of university credits.

I have two other future projects. The first involves investigating the relationship between psychotherapy and spiritual practice, and especially cooperating with therapists who also have experience of practice, in order to develop new therapeutic techniques for working with practitioners on the specific problems that can arise from practice. I have seen that often excessive expectations or unresolved personal conflicts best dealt with through psychotherapy can create problems for practitioners with their master, with other practitioners, and with the teaching.

The second involves working more closely with Native Americans. I have discovered that there are many similarities between the Native American spiritual traditions and Tibetan culture, particularly the Bon tradition. I would like to work more on sharing and exchanging information between these two spiritual cultures.

2

Tonpa Shenrab Miwoche and the History of Bon

Shenrab Miwoche

Bon is the ancient autochthonous pre-Buddhist religious tradition of Tibet, still practiced today by many Tibetans in Tibet and in India. The founder of the Bon religion in the human world is Lord Tonpa Shenrab Miwoche.

According to the traditional biographical account,[1] in a previous age Shenrab was called Salwa and studied the Bon doctrines with his two brothers Dagpa and Shepa in the Sidpa Yesang heaven under guidance of the Bon sage Bumtri Logi Cesan. After finishing their studies, the three brothers visited the God of Compassion, Shenlha Okar, to ask him how they could alleviate the suffering of sentient beings. Shenlha Okar advised them to act as guides to mankind in three successive world ages. Dagpa taught in the past world age; Salwa manifested as Tonpa Shenrab Miwoche and is the teacher and guide of the present world age; the youngest brother, Shepa, will come to teach in the next world age.

Tonpa Shenrab descended from the heavenly realms and manifested at the foot of Mount Meru with two of his closest disciples, Malo and Yulo. Then he took birth as a prince, the son of King Gyal Tokar and Queen Zanga Ringum, in a luminous garden full of marvellous flowers in a palace south of Mount Yungdrung Gutseg, at dawn on the eighth day of the first month of the first Wood Male Mouse year (1857 B.C.). He married while young and had children. At the age of thirty-one he renounced his worldly life and started to practice austerity and teach the Bon doctrine. Throughout his life, his efforts to propagate the Bon teachings were obstructed by the demon Khyabpa Lagring, who fought to destroy Shenrab's work; eventually he was converted and became Shenrab's disciple. Once, Khyabpa stole Shenrab's horses and Shenrab pursued him through Zhang Zhung into southern Tibet. Shenrab entered Tibet by crossing Mount Kongpo.[2]

This was Shenrab's only visit to Tibet. At that time the Tibetans practiced ritual sacrifice. Shenrab quelled the local demons and imparted instructions on the performance of rituals using offering cakes in the shapes of the sacrificial animals, which led to the Tibetans abandoning animal sacrifices. On the whole, he found the land unprepared to receive the five Ways "of the fruit" of the higher Bon teachings, so he taught the four Ways "of cause." In these practices the emphasis is on reinforcing relationships with the guardian spirits and the natural environment, exorcising demons, and eliminating negativities. He also taught practices of purification by fumigation and lustral sprinkling and introduced prayer flags as a way of reinforcing fortune and positive energy. Before leaving Tibet, he prophesied that all his teachings would flourish in Tibet when the time was ripe. Tonpa Shenrab passed away at the age of eighty-two.[3]

Mythological Origin and History of the Bon Religion

According to Bon mythological literature, there were three cycles of dissemination of the Bon doctrine, in three dimensions: the upper dimension of the gods, or *devas* (*lha*), the middle dimension of human beings (*mi*), and the lower dimension of the *nagas* (*klu*).

In the dimension of the *devas*, Shenrab built a temple called the "Indestructible Peak that is the Castle of the *Lha*" and opened the mandala of the "All-Victorious Ones of Space"; he established the Sutra teachings and appointed as his successor Dampa Togkar.

In the dimension of the *nagas*, he built a temple called the "Continent of the Hundred Thousand Gesars that is the Castle of the *Nagas*" and opened the mandala of the Pure Lotus Mother. He established the *Prajnaparamita Sutra* teachings and gave instructions on the nature of the mind.

In the human dimension, Shenrab sent emanations to three continents for the welfare of sentient beings. In this world, he originally expounded his teachings in the land of Olmo Lungring, situated to the west of Tibet and part of a larger country called Tazig, identified by some modern scholars as Persia or Tazikhistan. "*Ol*" symbolizes the unborn, "*mo*" the undiminishing, "*lung*" the prophetic words, and "*ring*" the everlasting compassion of Tonpa Shenrab. Olmo Lungring constitutes one third of the existing world and is formed like an eight-petalled lotus under a sky that appears as an eight-spoked wheel. In the center of Olmo Lungring rises Mount Yungdrung Gutseg "Nine Swastika Pyramid." The swastika is the symbol of permanence and indestructibility. The heaped nine swastikas represent the Nine Ways of Bon. At the base of Mount Yungdrung Gutseg spring four rivers, flowing in the four cardinal directions. This description has led some scholars to identify Mount Yungdrung Gutseg with Mount Kailash and Olmo Lungring with Zhang Zhung, the country lying around Mount Kailash in west Tibet and the cradle of Tibetan civilization. The mountain is surrounded by temples, cities, and parks. Access to Olmo Lungring is gained by the "arrow way," so named because, before visiting Tibet, Tonpa Shenrab shot an arrow and created a passage through the mountain range.

Until the seventh century, Zhang Zhung existed as a separate state comprising all of Western Tibet around Mount Kailash and Lake Manasarovar. The capital was Khyunglung Nulkhar, the "Silver Palace of the Garuda Valley," the ruins of which are to be found in Sutlej valley southwest of Mount Kailash. The people spoke a Tibeto-Burmese language and were ruled by a dynasty of kings that ended in the eighth century when King Ligmincha or Ligmirya

 སྟོན་པ་ཁྲི་གཏུག་རྒྱལ་བ་ལ་ན་མོ།། སྐུ་ལྷ་སྟོན་པ་ཡ་ནས།

Shenrab Miwo, Nirmanakaya form (Tonpa Trisug Gyalwa)

was assassinated by King Trisong Detsen of Tibet and Zhang Zhung was annexed to Tibet.

Further History of Bon

Bon underwent a decline in Tibet with the spread of Buddhism in Tibet and after the founding of the first Buddhist monastery at Samye in 779 during the reign of King Trisong Detsen. Although at first, King Trisong Detsen was reluctant to eliminate all Bon practices and even sponsored the translation of Bon texts, he later instigated a harsh repression of Bon. The great eighth-century Bon master and sage Dranpa Namkha, father of the Lotus born Guru Padmasambhava, founder of the Nyingmapa (*rNying ma pa*) Buddhist tradition and the master who spread the Tantric and Dzogchen teachings in Tibet, embraced the new religion in public but maintained his Bon practice and allegiance in private in order secretly to preserve Bon. He asked the king "Why do you make a distinction between *bon* and *chos*?" (The word *bon* for the Bonpas and *chos* for the Buddhists both mean "dharma," or "truth"), since he held that in essence they were the same. Vairochana, the Buddhist scholar and disciple of Padmasambhava, and many other translators of Indian and Oddiyana Buddhist texts participated in the translation of Bon texts from the language of Drusha. To be saved from destruction, many of the Bon texts had to be hidden as *termas* so that they could be rediscovered later in more propitious times.

In the ninth and tenth centuries, Bon suffered further persecutions and attempts to eradicate it. Followers of Bon, however, were able to preserve the scriptures until the eleventh century during which time there was a Bon revival. This was precipitated by the rediscovery of several important texts by Shenchen Luga, a descendant of the great master Tonpa Shenrab himself.

Shenchen Luga had many followers, some of whom founded the first Bon monasteries in Tibet. In 1405, the great Bon master Nyamed Sherab Gyaltsen founded Menri Monastery. Menri and Yundgrung Ling Monastery became the most important of the Bon monasteries.

Notes to Chapter 2

[1] There are three different editions of his biography: the long version, called *'Dus pa rin po che'i rgyud dri ma med pa gzi brjid rab tu 'bar ba'i mdo*, consists of sixty-one chapters in twelve volumes (partly translated by Snellgrove in *The Nine Ways of Bon*). The medium version, called *'Dus pa rin po che'i rgyud gzer mig*, consists of eighteen chapters in two volumes. The short version, called *mDo 'dus*, consists of twenty-four chapters in one volume.

[2] Kongpo Bonri (The Mountain of Bon); it is the only sacred mountain in Tibet which both Bonpos and Buddhists circumambulate counterclockwise. The mountain has many remarkable features, including rocks on which are carved descriptions and scenes from Shenrab's life. (I visited this sacred mountain in 1986 and noticed hundreds of Tibetans, Bonpos, and Buddhists alike, completing the three-day circumambulation of the mountain.)

[3] After Shenrab's death, six great translators studied and trained under his successor Mucho Demdrug and subsequently translated the Bon teachings into their own languages. These six translators were Mutsa Traher from Tazig, Tritag Patsa from Zhang Zhung, Guhu Lipa from Sumpa, Ladag Nagdro from China, and Sertog Lejam from Khrom. Some of the teachings that originated in Tazig were directly introduced into Tibet, while others were brought into Tibet through Zhang Zhung, India, and China. The teachings that came from India are known as *Gyagarma* and contain all the cycles of the *Nine Ways of the Central Treasure*.

3

The Bon Doctrine

Different Presentations of the Bon Teachings

The Bon teachings imparted by Tonpa Shenrab are presented in various ways and with different classifications in the three written accounts of Tonpa Shenrab's life. Shenrab is said to have expounded Bon in three successive cycles of teachings: first he expounded the "Nine Ways (or successive stages of practice) of Bon"; then he taught the "Four Bon Portals and the Fifth, the Treasury"; finally he revealed the "Outer, Inner, and Secret Precepts."

The First Cycle: The Nine Ways

There are three different ways of classifying the Nine Ways of Everlasting Bon: the Southern, Northern, and Central Treasures. These are systems of teachings that were hidden during early persecutions of Bon to be later rediscovered as *termas*. The *termas* rediscovered in Drigtsam thakar (Brig mtshams mtha' dkar) in south Tibet and in Padro (sPa gro) in Bhutan constitute the Southern

Treasures; those rediscovered in Zang zang lha dag and in Dangra khyung dzong (Dwang ra khyung rdzong) in north Tibet constitute the Northern Treasures; those rediscovered at Samye (bSam yas) and in Yerpe Drak (Yer pa'i brag) in central Tibet constitute the Central Treasures.

In the Southern Treasures, the Nine Ways are subdivided into the lower "Four Ways of Cause," which contain the myths, legends, rituals and practices concerned mainly with working with energy in terms of magic for healing and prosperity, and the higher "Five Ways of the Fruit," the purpose of which is to liberate the practitioner from the cycle of samsaric transmigration.

The Nine Ways of the Northern Treasures are not widely known. In the Zang zang ma system, they are divided in three groups: external, internal, and secret.

The Nine Ways of the Central Treasures are very similar to the Nine Ways found in Nyingmapa Buddhism. In fact, they are cycles of *Gyagarma* teachings that were introduced into Tibet from India and were translated by the great scholar Vairochana, who worked as translator in both the Bon and Buddhist spiritual traditions.

The Second Cycle: The Four Portals and the One Treasury

The second cycle of Bon expounded by Shenrab is divided into five parts. The first portal deals with esoteric Tantric practices and spells. The second portal consists of various rituals (magical, prognosticatory, and divinitory, etc.) for purification. The third relates rules for monastic discipline and lay people, with philosophical explanation, and the fourth instructs on psycho-spiritual exercises such as Dzogchen meditation. The fifth teaching is called the One Treasury and comprises the essential aspects of all four portals.

The Final Cycle: Outer, Inner, and Secret Precepts

The final teachings expounded by Tonpa Shenrab consist in the three cycles of Outer, Inner, and Secret Precepts.

The outer cycle is the path of renunciation (*spong lam*), the Sutra teachings. The inner cycle is the path of transformation (*sgyur lam*), the Tantric teachings, which use mantras. The secret cycle is the path of self-liberation (*grol lam*), the Dzogchen teachings.

This division into Sutra, Tantra, and Dzogchen (*mdo sngags sems gsum*) is also found in Tibetan Buddhism.

Sutra, Tantra, and Dzogchen

According to Bon, the five passions—ignorance, attachment, anger, jealousy, and pride—are the principal cause of all the problems of this life and of transmigration in samsara. They are also called the five poisons because they kill people. These are the passions that we must overcome through practice. According to the Sutra view, it takes many lifetimes to purify the passions and achieve enlightenment, whereas according to the Tantric and the Dzogchen views the practitioner can attain enlightenment in this very lifetime.

Different religions and spiritual traditions have devised various ways of purifying the passions and attaining realization. In Yungdrung Bon, these are the method of renunciation, the method of transformation, and the method of self-liberation.

For dealing with the passions, we can use the example of a poisonous plant. According to the Sutra interpretation, the plant must be destroyed, because there is no other way to resolve the problem of its poison. The Sutra practitioner renounces all the passions.

According to the Tantric system, the tantric adept should take the poisonous plant and mix it with another plant in order to form an antidote: he does not reject the passions but tries to transform them into aids to practice. The Tantric adept is like a doctor who transforms the poisonous plants into medicine.

The peacock, on the other hand, eats the poisonous plant because he has the capacity to use the energy contained in the poison to make himself more beautiful; that is, he frees the poisonous property of the plant into energy for growth. This is the Dzogchen method of effortlessly liberating passions directly as they arise.

4

Bonpo Dzogchen

Self-arising wisdom is the base.
The five negative emotions are manifested energy.
Seeing emotions as mistaken is an error.
Letting them be in their nature is the method
To find the non-dual state of Liberation.
Overcoming hope and fear is the result.

Although there have been practitioners of Dzogchen in all the Tibetan religious traditions, such as the Fifth Dalai Lama of the Gelugpa school, the Third Karmapa Rangjung Dorje of the Kagyupa school and Drakpa Gyaltsen of the Sakyapa school, the most important lineages of the Dzogchen teachings are found in Bon, the native religion of Tibet, and in the Nyingmapa (oldest) Tibetan Buddhist school. Both these traditions classify their teachings in "nine Ways," or paths of practice leading to enlightenment or realization, and in both classifications, Dzogchen is the ninth and highest Way.

Nowadays, masters of all the Tibetan sects have started to teach Dzogchen, and Dzogchen seems almost to be becoming a kind of fashion in the West.

Dzogchen

Dzogchen (*rdzogs chen*) literally means "perfection," "accomplishment," or "fulfillment" (*rdzogs*) that is "complete" or "great" (*chen*). Although Dzogchen is the "single great sphere," for convenience it is described as having the three aspects of base, path, and fruit: "base" because the ground of Dzogchen is the primordial state of the individual; "path" because Dzogchen is the supreme direct and immediate path to realization; and "fruit" because Dzogchen is the consummation of enlightenment, liberation from the cycle of illusory samsaric transmigration in one single lifetime.

In order better to understand Dzogchen, let us look further at the division into base, path, and fruit.

According to the Dzogchen teaching, the essence (*ngo bo*) of the base of everything (*kun gzhi*) is empty (*ston pa nyid*) and primordially pure (*ka dag*); the nature (*rang bzhin*) of the base is clarity (*gsal ba*) that is spontaneously perfected (*lhun sgrub*); the inseparable union (*dbyer med*) of the primordially pure essence and the spontaneously perfected nature is the unobstructed (*ma 'gag pa*) flow of energy or compassion (*thugs rje*). In the individual mind, this base is the natural state (*gzhi*) and is the source of samsara for the deluded mind (*ma rig pa*) and of nirvana for the mind in which knowledge (*rig pa*) is awakened.

The essence of the *kunzhi*, or base, is called the mother (*ma*), awakened awareness (*rig pa*) is called the son (*bu*), and the inseparability (*dbyer med*) of mother and son is the flow of energy (*rtsal*).

The path (*lam*) consists of gaining insight into the view (*lta ba*) of Dzogchen, which is knowledge of the true condition of the base of the individual, and making the flow of *rigpa*, cultivated through meditation, continuous in the post-meditation period so that it can be integrated in our behavior or attitude and activities in everyday life.

The fruit is the actualization of the inherent three *kayas* in this very lifetime and culminates in the attainment of the rainbow or light body at the end of life, whereby at death the material body leaves no mortal remains but dissolves into its nature, which is light.

Dzogchen in the Context of Bon Spiritual Practice

Dzogchen is the highest spiritual tradition in Bon. In the past, the practitioners who knew and practiced Dzogchen in Tibet were few, even within the Bon and Nyingma traditions. One reason for this was that it was not easy to receive these teachings: they were kept very secret, few masters gave them, and to few students. Even in current times, lay Bon adepts in Tibet habitually spend a lot of time performing the nine preliminary (*ngondro*) practices and the *powa*, while monks who stay in monasteries engage mainly in intellectual and philosophical study and debate, and recitation of ritual and liturgical texts.

Many masters insisted (and many masters now continue to insist) that practitioners complete the *ngondro* practices before being given Dzogchen teachings. These preliminary practices are described in the *Nyams rgyud rgyal ba'i phyag khrid*. Each of these nine practices must be performed one hundred thousand times. The nine practices are:

1. The generation of compassion for all sentient beings
2. Taking refuge
3. Offering the mandala
4. Meditation on impermanence
5. Confession of transgressions
6. Making prostrations
7. Guru yoga, merging the mind with the enlightened mind of the guru visualized in front of oneself
8. Offering prayers
9. Receiving blessings

However, when I received the *Zhang Zhung Nyan Gyud* teachings, Lopon Sangye Tenzin maintained that although keeping the Dzogchen teachings secret may have been suitable in ancient times, in our own troubled times it is better to give them more openly and freely (but without lessening their value in this way), or there is the danger that they will die out.

Dzogchen in Bon and Nyingmapa

We have seen that Dzogchen is common to Bon and Nyingmapa Buddhism, and that these two spiritual traditions also have in common a nine-fold division of their Ways, or modes of religious observance. However, there are major differences between the respective divisions in nine Ways of the Bonpos and the Nyingmapas. It is worth noting that there are six, and not nine, grades of practice in the other Tibetan Buddhist schools: Kagyupa, Sakyapa, and Gelugpa, who adhere to the new tradition (*gsar ma*) of the later translations of the Buddhist canon undertaken during the second spread of Buddhism in Tibet in the tenth and eleventh centuries. The nine Ways of the Buddhists comprise only traditional Buddhist material, and strictly speaking (as Professor Snellgrove has pointed out) the two lower paths, pertaining to Hinayana Buddhism, are practically irrelevant to Tibetan Buddhist religious practices that are grounded in Mahayana Buddhism. In contrast, the nine Ways of the Bonpos as well as practices of Buddhist origin comprehend the entire compass of indigenous Tibetan customs and religious beliefs and practices, including medical science, astrology and cosmology, sortilege and prediction, appeasement and exorcism of powerful evil spirits and ghosts, rites for prosperity and tantric rites of destruction of enemies, ransom and guidance of the dead, moral discipline for lay and monastic practitioners, Tantric practices and rites, hagiography, and the highest spiritual path of Dzogchen. In this respect, Bon may be said to be the true religion of Tibet, embracing both autochthonous and imported religious observances.

There are also many points in common between Bon and Nyingmapa Buddhism. As noted, both uphold and propagate in an official way the transmission of the Dzogchen teachings, which are found only sporadically in gifted individual practitioners of the other Tibetan traditions that do not have specific lineages of Dzogchen masters. Both worship Kuntuzangpo as the supreme primordial Adibuddha, while the other three schools of Tibetan Buddhism worship Vajradhara as Adibuddha, and both have a *terma* tradition of concealed spiritual treasures rediscovered by *tertons* (personages prophesied to reveal the *terma* in propitious times). In fact, many famous *tertons* belonged to both traditions.

Furthermore, the Nyingmapas are the only Tibetan Buddhists to openly acknowledge as Buddhist those teachings of non-Indian origin that were spread during the first introduction of Buddhism into Tibet during the reign of King Songtsen Gampo and later in the eighth century by the charismatic master Padmasambhava and his associates. These teachings include currents of Buddhist teachings coming from China and central Asia as well as from India. In the second spread of Buddhism in Tibet in the tenth and eleventh centuries, all Buddhist teachings of which an Indian origination could not be verified were excluded from the Buddhist canon rendered official by the other three later schools of Tibetan Buddhism. The Bonpos maintain that, as Buddha Sakyamuni was a disciple of Tonpa Shenrab Miwoche, all Buddhist teachings, whether originating in India or elsewhere, are in fact teachings of everlasting Bon.

Three Streams of Dzogchen in Bon

In Bon, Dzogchen has traditionally been divided in three streams known collectively as *A rdzogs snyan rgyud*, i.e. *Ati*, Dzogchen and *Zhang Zhung Nyan Gyud*. The first two are *terma* traditions based on rediscovered texts while the third is an oral tradition based on continuous transmission by an uninterrupted lineage of masters.

The *Ati* system was founded in the eleventh century by Dampa (Holy Man) Meu Gongjad Ritro Chenpo (1038-1096), who extracted the original teachings from the *Khro rgyud* cycle of teachings by Tonpa Shenrab.[1]

Literally *Ati* means "Guide of *A*." *A* represents the unconditioned primordial state, the natural state of the mind; it is white to represent the innate purity of the mind. The practitioner engages in *zhiné* practice, starting with fixation using the Tibetan letter *A* to focus concentration, in order to develop insight and experience the natural state of the mind. It corresponds to the *semde* series of Dzogchen teachings of the Nyingmapa Buddhist tradition, connected with the mind.

The name "rDzogs chen" given to the second stream does not refer to Dzogchen in its general meaning but instead denotes a particular type of Dzogchen teaching with its own specific lineage.[2] This system corresponds to the *longde* series in Nyingmapa Dzogchen, connected with clarity and space.

The third stream comprises the Dzogchen teachings of the *Zhang Zhung Nyan Gyud*, the Oral Transmission of Zhang Zhung, the oldest and most important Dzogchen tradition and meditation system in Bon. This series of teachings was systematized by the Zhang Zhung master Gyerpung Nangzher Lodpo, who received them from his master Tapihritsa in the eighth century. However, as we shall see below, these teachings were not composed by their human founder: they are not fabricated by thought but are self-originated. They have enjoyed continuous transmission by a "long" lineage through the centuries and never had to be concealed and rediscovered as *terma* which have "short," or direct transmission from the time of their revelation. This stream of teachings corresponds to the Upadesha series in Nyingmapa Dzogchen, the series of "secret instructions."

Although all three streams of Dzogchen have their own preliminary practices and lineages of masters of the transmission, the essence and purpose of all three is the same: introduction to the natural state of Dzogchen. Some lineage masters hold all three transmissions. In Tibet this transmission from master to disciple, who in his turn becomes the master who transmits the teaching to his own disciple, is called "hot" because the personal transmission of direct experience protects it, so that it remains alive without becoming something cold and merely intellectual, derived from books and conceptual thought.

Tapihritsa

In the Bon tradition, we do the practice of guru yoga, of blending our mind with the natural mind of the guru visualized as the deity Shenlha Okar or the figure of Tapihritsa, who represent the union of all the Bon lineage masters. Tapihritsa is depicted in Dharmakaya form, like Kuntuzangpo, naked and without ornaments.

According to the traditional account in the *Zhang Zhung Nyan Gyud*, Tapihritsa was born in the eighth century. His father was Rasang Lugyal and his mother was Sherig Sal. He received teachings through the telepathic-mind and oral transmissions from his father and from the great master Ponchen Rasang, but in particular he was the disciple of the Siddha and twenty-fourth lineage master of the oral transmission of Zhang Zhung Tsepung, Lawa

Gyaltsen. He practiced austerity for nine years on the rocky mountain Tagtab Sengei Drag, during which time the silence was never broken by human speech, and obtained the ordinary and supreme attainments. At the end of his life, he achieved the rainbow body, entering the totally purified condition without leaving physical remains. For himself he realized the state of *bonku*, for others the state of *tulku*, manifesting in visible form to reawaken those who had the blessing of seeing him. His physical manifestation was not limited and he had the capacity to transform into different shapes. After obtaining the rainbow body, Tapihritsa reincarnated as a child to teach his two main disciples, Gyerpung Nangzher Lodpo and Mo Yungdrung.

Gyerpung Nangzher Lodpo belonged to the illustrious Gurib family, a clan that boasted several previous lineage holders. His father was Gurib Bumed, his mother Mangorza Droma. He received instructions and teachings from the master Zepung Lawa Gyaltsen and from many scholars. He was a great scholar, perfectly versed in all the doctrines of the nine Ways. He practiced austerity and kept all the vows. He obtained great power through the practice of the Yidam Meri and became royal priest to King Ligmincha of Zhang Zhung. After the murder of King Ligmincha by King Trisong Detsen of Tibet, he hurled magic bombs at Trisong Detsen, thereby saving the Bon teachings by forcing the Tibetan king to refrain from destroying the Bon texts, so that the *Zhang Zhung Nyan|Gyud* texts, which he had compiled, did not have to be hidden and rediscovered as *terma*.

Nangzher Lodpo had become very proud because of his great power and fame, and it was to overcome his pride that Tapihritsa appeared to him in the form of a child and released him from all the chains of his attachment to ego, whereby he was able to contemplate his mind in the condition of equipoise and achieve perfect supreme realization and became an omniscient Buddha.

The child Tapihritsa came to Mo Yungdrung, who was very wealthy, and told him he was begging because he could not find any work, so the rich practitioner offered to let him stay with his family as a servant looking after the animals. The boy was very intelligent and sharp in his work and was given the name Nyeleg. At that time, Nangzher Lodpo was in retreat in a nearby cave, sponsored by Mo Yungdrung. One day Nyeleg was returning with his bag from taking the animals to graze in the mountains when he saw Nangzher Lodpo come out of his cave. Nyeleg prostrated and paid ninefold respect in the traditional way. The master noticed that the boy was trained in the doctrine and asked him, "Who is your master? What meditation do you practice? What are you carrying in your bag? Why are you behaving this way? Where are you going?"

Nyeleg answered, "The view is my master. I practice the nonconceptual state. I meditate on everything I see in the three dimensions (of existence). I am carrying thoughts in my bag. My behavior is to work as the servant of sentient beings. I am going nowhere." The master was disappointed. He felt proud of being an important master and felt that the child's answer had been disrespectful. He rejoined skeptically, "If the view is your master, it means you have no master. If the nonconceptual state is your practice, it means you don't need food and clothes. If your meditation is all the visions of the three dimensions, it means you don't need to meditate: without meditating you will obtain complete realization. If you are carrying thoughts in your bag, it means you don't have desires." So the boy said, "If you do not understand view as the master, then who taught the primordial Buddha?" He meant that in order to understand the true condition, there is no need of a master; the master explains and confirms to the practitioner his experience of his own innate wisdom, something the practitioner already knows; there is nothing new that he can teach him. "My practice is the nonconceptual state because in this base there are no thoughts: conceptual views are not meditation practice. My meditation is the visions of the three worlds: in the true nature there is no bias. If there were, it would not be meditation. If I am carrying thoughts in my bag, it means that desires are finished, so there are no thoughts. If you have no concepts, you understand the meaning. If my practice is to be the servant of all beings, it means all the experiences of bliss and suffering are of one taste, and experiencing the nonseparation of good and bad is my practice." Nangzher Lodpo became annoyed and said, "If you are so intelligent, tomorrow we must debate in front of the king." The boy laughed loudly and said, "Cause and effect is ignorant understanding. Great meditators who keep thoughts imprisoned and controlled are drowsy and sleep when they meditate. Language and the logic of philosophy are like weapons and dark nets. Debating is only verbal concepts and Tantric practice is transforming the mind and not leaving it in its nature. Learned scholars have meaningless understanding, and their view and meditation are like bubbles, mere words without application in practice. All these are not real practice; the ultimate state is unconditioned. There is no practice to do, there are no obscurations, and once you have true understanding there is no more that has to be forced or changed."

There are three ways of explaining things to people: you can point out their mistakes to them, which is not the best way; you can remain silent, because if people ask many questions and you do not answer, they may understand something that way; or you can act the same way they do. This is what Nyeleg was doing: he was reacting to the questions and answers he was receiving. He was criticizing Nangzher Lodpo, who got angry and said, "Tomorrow we will debate in front of the king. If you win, you will become my master; if I win, I will punish you." Then suddenly Nangzher Lodpo recognized the boy as an emanation and fell unconscious. When he regained consciousness, he confessed his negative acts to Tapihritsa. Meanwhile, as all the animals were wandering loose and being eaten by wolves, Mo Yungdrung came and started berating the child, but Nangzher Lodpo told him, "You should not get angry because he is a great master and is very important for us." So they both were upset and apologized for the way they had spoken to the boy and then fainted. When they regained their senses, Tapihritsa had risen into the sky and was sitting in space, surrounded by rainbow circles and laughing. Then the two disciples sat down and Tapihritsa started to impart his last teaching. Although Nangzher Lodpo was very learned, his great pride was still blocking true understanding, and these short but essential teachings helped him to liberate himself.

Nangzher Lodpo's Invocation of Tapihritsa

Nangzher Lodpo chanted the following invocation to Tapihritsa:

> E ma ho!
> How wonderful!
> You are the manifestation of the primordial base.

Your body appears like a white luminous crystal,
Clear and without impurities,
And spreads rays of light in the ten directions.
You are naked, without ornaments:
This is the innermost sense of the primordial state.
Endowed with the twofold wisdom of emptiness and
    skillful means
With compassion you think of the benefit of beings.
With precision you teach
The supreme teaching of the Great Perfection,
The essence of the awareness of the realized ones,
Peak of the way of realization,
Heart of the revealed texts (*tantra*), of their essential
Summaries (*lung*), and of the secret instructions
    (*upadesa*);
With clarity you point out
The true condition of the base of the universe
From which arise enlightenment and transmigration,
Liberation and illusion,
The sound, lights, and rays, defects and qualities.
Dispelling the darkness of beings' intellect
You enable us instantly to realize contemplative
    experience
And bring about the resolution in the mind's emptiness
Of the duality of transmigration and enlightenment;
You enable us to reach the ultimate condition
Of the three supreme dimensions.
With concentration, with devotion I pray to you
    Tapihritsa,
Protector of beings:
Confer the initiation and grant the empowerment to
    me and other beings.
May the external, internal, and secret obstacles be
    eliminated
And may the delusory notion of ego,
That constitutes the illusion of ignorance,
Be dissolved.
Having realized pure awareness of presence
May contemplation and activity be brought to fulfillment.
I pray to you, grant me now

Understanding of the great meaning beyond the intellect
Of the primordial (baseless) emptiness.
I address my invocation to Tapihritsa, Lord of Beings:
May the beings of the six realms be protected by your compassion
And may my mind be liberated!

Tapihritsa's Final Instructions

First Tapihritsa granted the instruction on the "Four Goodnesses":

1. View: By omnipervasiveness, let unconditioned self-awareness go into the self-liberated vision not grasped by mind; this way is good.
2. Meditation: Let baseless experience unconditionally perceive the nonreferential and self-clear meditation; this way is good.
3. Behavior: Without dualistic choosing, let experiential vision directly perform flexible actions which are without attachment; this way is good.
4. Fruit: Let the limits of hope and fear self-liberate into the unobtainable self-arising realization; this way is good.

After giving this teaching, Tapihritsa was silent for a moment, then continued with the teaching on the "Four Applications of Practice":

1. You cannot practice the nature of phenomena; apply the nonpractice state of the nature of phenomena.
2. You cannot understand the Dharmakaya by the cause and effect (logic) of the mind; apply the mind that is beyond cause and secondary causes.
3. You cannot find the essential knowledge; apply that which you cannot find.
4. You cannot change by trying; apply the immutable state.

Then after sitting in silent contemplation, Tapihritsa taught the "Five Applications of Practice":

1. Because the natural condition is without bias, there is unconditioned arising; apply the practice that is unconditioned and without bias.

2. Because there is no desire and attachment to objects, there is self-liberation without liberation from objects; apply the practice that is beyond bondage and release.

3. Because the mind is without birth and death, there is abiding in the unborn nature; apply the practice that is beyond filling and emptying.

4. Because there are no words and expressions, there is abiding in the space of silence; apply the practice that is beyond development and decline.

5. From the beginning, there is no separation from the natural condition and no relation to external vision; apply the practice that is beyond separation and relation.

Tapihritsa said, "Observe yourself. Do you have this knowledge in yourself or not?" He remained silently in contemplation, then after a while he spoke again and taught the "Four Trainings of the Nature":

1. Apply contemplation without time limits; abide in the nature which is beyond time.

2. Apply undistracted contemplation; abide without distraction in the nature of the space of great bliss.

3. Apply contemplation without interruption; abide in the self-born, natural condition that is without interruption.

4. Apply the state beyond birth and death in the essential nature; abide in the unborn single nature.

Tapihritsa remained in silent contemplation for some time and asked again "Observe yourself to see if you have this knowledge in yourself." Then after a moment, he taught the "Three Certainties":

1. By understanding that there is no independent existence, you attain the certainty of single understanding.

2. By understanding nonduality, you attain the certainty of single taste.

3. By understanding nondirectionality, you attain the certainty of boundlessness.

He added, "If you attain these three certainties, you are a yogi."

It was in order to give these important teachings to his disciple Nangzher Lodpo that Tapihritsa had taken rebirth as a child. He continued, "These teachings will frighten people with limited out-look. They cannot be understood by the ordinary rational mind. Hide these teachings in the secret place in your mind." He concluded, "If you always remember me, you will meet me; if you forget me, you will never meet me."

Nangzher Lodpo and Mo Yungdrung started to write down these teachings, the last given by Tapihritsa, and they became famous and respected in the Bon tradition because they were the first to leave written records of the teachings. This is the origin of the *Zhang Zhung Nyan Gyud* teachings that have been handed down to us to the present day.

Notes to Chapter 4

[1] Together with the *Zhi ba don gyi skor*, these formed the *sPyi spungs yan lag gi skor* cycle of teachings. Meu Gongjad added his own *gongter* (*dgongs gter*, spiritual mind treasures) and composed a cycle of eighty meditation periods of one or two weeks, called *A khrid thun mtshams brgyad cu pa*, in three sections, comprising instructions on view, or *tawa* (*lta ba*), meditation, or *gompa* (*sgom pa*), and behavior, or *chopa* (*spyod pa*): on completion of the course, the adept was styled *togden* (*rtogs ldan*). In the thirteenth century, the master Aza Lodro Gyaltsen (1198-1263) reduced the system to thirty periods, and subsequently the "Venerable Hermit" Druchen Gyalwa Yungdrung (1242-1296) reduced it further to fifteen sessions, and since this time the system has been known as *The Fifteen-Session A-khrid of Dru* (*Bru'i a khrid thun mtshams bco lnga pa*). In the present century, the Bon master Shardza Rinpoche (1859-1934; this master achieved the light body) wrote a commentary on the *Ati* and the dark retreat (*mun mtshams*) and contributed to its further development.

[2] It was founded in 1088 A.D by the *terton* Zhoton Nogrub Drakpa (gZhod ston dNgos grub grags pa) when he rediscovered a group of *termas* called *Great Expanse of the Zenith of the Great Perfection* (*bLa med rDzogs chen yang rtse klong chen*) hidden by the eighth-century Bonpo master Nyachen Lishu Tagring (sNya chen Li shu stag rings) behind a statue of Vairochana in Khomting (Khom thing) temple in Lodrag (Lho drag).

5

How and Why to Practice

The principal aim and final result of practicing is
   realization.
The secondary results of the practice
Are to remove all the obstacles from our minds
So that we lead better, more calm, and more peaceful
   lives,
   In order to have the opportunity to practice.

I think that we should be happy to have come into contact with
spiritual teachings and to be able to receive teachings and explanations in such a direct way. It is good that we appreciate their
value and that we have the opportunity and the willingness to
practice them. But merely to acknowledge the positive value of
the teachings is not enough; it is also necessary to have the intention to practice them, and then to execute that intention. Once we
start to follow and practice the teachings, they should become the
main concern of our life, the most important thing we possess.

Deciding to Follow a Spiritual Path

Before we decide to follow a path of spiritual teaching, whatever the culture or creed from which it came, it is necessary to investigate our motivation for doing so. The main reason we become interested in following a teaching is not because we have nothing else to do, or because we need to keep busy, but because we want something different in our lives from what we see around us. When we discover the way "normal" people (who find nothing important in their existence) live, and when we see that the activities with which we have become accustomed to filling our lives do not solve the problem of the suffering that our existence in the cycle of samsara brings us, we realize we have to do something different from our everyday life. Most people do not try to understand these things, and what lies beyond their understanding does not exist for them. What we as spiritual practitioners are trying to discover, what we are trying to do, has no interest for them. They do not believe anything they cannot see with the naked eye. We must avoid such an extreme of blindness, but neither should our spiritual quest become a kind of spiritual fantasy, a way of avoiding everyday reality.

In order to practice, it is important first of all to understand death and rebirth, as it is through awareness of the cycle of suffering that we first approach the teaching. Through investigation we can realize that our human existence, our precious human birth, gives us a great opportunity, since through our contact with the teachings we can learn how to use our intelligence to examine our thoughts and observe how they give rise to our attachment, and we can discover how to bring our grasping and the consequent cycle of suffering to an end.

Incidentally, spiritual teachings are not limited to the human dimension; even animals may practice and achieve realization. In fact, there are stories of masters who were able to communicate with animals and who transmitted teachings to them. For example, there is a story about one such master at the beginning of this century who used to communicate with yetis, goats, and pigeons. One day a pigeon came to the tent where this master was giving a teaching. The master interrupted the teaching and went outside, sat down in front of the pigeon, and communicated with it without words. The bird was very weak and could not sit in the right posture, so the master put some rice in a bowl and set the bird in a nook in the rice so that it could assume the meditation position. After receiving teachings in the correct meditation posture for a few moments, the pigeon died and attained liberation.

Human or animal, in order to bring the cycle of samsara to an end, we must discover the source of suffering. This is the thinking mind that gives rise to the passions and to attachment. The only way to overcome the poisons of the five passions and their manifestations is to bring the mind under control. This can be done through practicing the teachings that bid us to observe ourselves in order to understand and, through practice, overcome our grasping mind. In this way the teachings guide us to know the underlying nature of the mind and integrate its true condition with our daily life.

But many people, critical of Dzogchen, question why we need to practice at all if, as according to Dzogchen, the primordial state is already the enlightened state. If our true nature is already Buddhahood, what is the need to cultivate enlightenment? We cannot side-step these criticisms since, according to Dzogchen, Buddhahood is indeed our natural state; we do not create it, but simply discover it through our meditation. But if we simply agree with our critics, this would mean there is no need to practice. These are important things to think about. We must answer that although the natural state of the mind is primordially pure, there are two ways of being pure. Defilements, or obscurations, are not in the nature of the mind (*sems nyid*) but in the moving mind (*sems*), so they can be purified. It is as in the Tibetan story of the old beggar woman who slept on a pillow of gold every night: she was rich, but since she did not appreciate the value of gold, she thought she was poor. In the same way, the primordial purity of our mind is of no use to us if we are not aware of it and do not integrate it with our moving mind. If we realize our innate purity but only integrate with it from time to time, we are not totally realized. Being in total integration all the time is final realization. But many people prefer thinking and speaking about integration to actualizing it.

Often, Dzogchen practitioners say, "You cannot think or talk about Dzogchen because it is ineffable." But it is not like that: Dzogchen experience is beyond thoughts and words, but we practitioners are not beyond doubts and questions, and we need to have them resolved. We cannot simply say, "I am a Dzogchen practitioner, I don't want to have doubts." Saying this is not enough to get rid of them, so it is important to think about these matters, otherwise we will remain in the state of doubt and not achieve the pure state. For example in Dzogchen, if we say that our natural state is spontaneously perfected, we mean that we already have the quality of realization in ourselves and that it is not something we have to get from outside. But even though it is a quality that is innate, we have to develop it. The traditional analogy is to the way the quality of butter already exists in milk: to get the butter we have to churn the milk.

Choosing a Path

When we decide that we want to follow a spiritual path, usually we choose teachings that we think will be beneficial for us, but often we make this choice in a very limited way, according to how we feel at the time or according to what path we find intellectually stimulating; or else we have a limited idea of what we feel is important for us according to the circumstances when we choose to practice. When our feelings or our ideas or the circumstances change, we change our practice. In this way we are continually changing practices and finally get fed up because nothing happens and nothing seems to work. So it is important not to seek and view teachings in this way and instead of choosing practices because of circumstances, we should try to be aware of what the long-term benefits are of the various practices. For example, Tibetans do many practices for wealth and long life, and sometimes it can be very important to do such practices, but they are not the main practices, and particularly not so in Dzogchen. It is more important to understand the fundamental aim and meaning of the teachings and then to apply them.

Before putting into practice the meditation instructions we receive, it is necessary and important to listen to the teachings we receive in the correct way. One of the major problems beginners have is that they receive many different teachings, as if they were throwing a lot of mail into a big post-bag. What then happens is that the letter they want, the specific teaching they need at a particular moment, might be at the bottom of the bag. It is important instead to know exactly where to put each part of the teachings we receive: this means knowing which stage of practice we have reached, what understanding we have, and which practices to apply. We cannot, and should not, start by trying indiscriminately to practice everything. And it is important to relate what we hear to our own personal experience: there is nothing, not even the most profound explanation of the three *kayas* (Dharmakaya, Sambhogakaya, Nirmanakaya), that we cannot relate to our own selves. We must understand what the terms used in the teachings refer to through our own practice and relate them to our own experience.

Once we decide to follow a master, it is important to respect him. Often before giving disciples teachings, the master will ask them to work for him, cooking and cleaning and doing other things as a kind of purification. Then when we receive teachings from the master, we should practice them until we realize their goal.

Dealing with Confusion About Practice

We have seen that sometimes practitioners change practices and teachers. If we do not have the direct experience and understanding of the fundamental base within ourselves as the foundation of our practice, then our understanding will be something constructed by the moving mind, and what we then change is the form of the practice. If we have a form, we can change it in different ways, but in terms of the real sense of the practice, there is nothing to change. Once we have realized that, any changes we make will not have a negative influence either on our lives or on the practices we do. Otherwise, varying the practices we do will only add to the confusion of our lives.

Normally, of course, there is confusion in our lives in terms of our work and our relationships with other people. But in regards to the teaching, confusion often leads us to rely too much on the master: we do not try to see things by ourselves but instead give complete responsibility to another person. Even concerning our daily lives we ask the teacher what we should do and where we should go! We become too dependent, and when our lives do not work out the way we want, we change practices and teachers. This process repeats itself continually and nothing very profound ever happens, and in the end we may feel we have wasted our time by practicing. In a way this is true, as we have tried to do something positive and in the end have achieved nothing; but this is because we have approached the practice in the wrong way, without first establishing a foundation. It should not be this way, because in undertaking a practice we are trying to bring some benefit and peace to our minds. The principal aim and final result of practicing is realization. The secondary results of the practice are to remove all the obstacles from our minds so that we lead better, more calm, and more peaceful lives in order to have the opportunity to practice. Otherwise, final realization is very far away. Unless we know how to apply these practices in our daily lives, they will be of very little help to us. So it is important on entering into the teaching and becoming practitioners to learn to apply the practices in a simple way, without having any confusion in ourselves about the fundamental base of the individual. We must know ourselves, through the direct experience of our own mind and our own natural state rather than knowing in a theoretical way what the teachings say about the base.

According to the Dzogchen teachings, the fundamental base of the individual, understood by insight gained through practice, is the inseparability of clarity and emptiness in the primordial state or natural condition. We are introduced to this understanding through our experience of practice, which is confirmed by the master's teachings and explanations, and we try to develop it further through the practice of meditation. Meditation is practiced in all spiritual paths, and focused concentration in the early stages of the path and conceptless and focusless contemplation in the later stages constitute the path of Dzogchen. The later contemplation practices particular to Dzogchen are *trekchö* and *tögel*; however, before embarking on these practices, it is necessary to have established a firm base in meditation through concentration practice.

The Right Order of Practices

The *ngondro,* or "preliminary practices," are generally completed as a preparation for receiving teachings. However, it is important not to treat them as merely formal practices that we must repeat 100,000 times, otherwise we will not get into the real sense of the *ngondro* and cannot achieve their real purpose. Doing the *ngondro* is important because these practices of confession, purification, generosity, meditation on death and impermanence, guru yoga, etc. also serve to prepare the practitioner. They correct the practitioner's being by removing the strong ego formed by the five passions. It is necessary to do this because only then are we ready to receive the teachings in a pure way, like a clean vessel ready to receive the "lion's milk," the precious liquid of the teachings. Otherwise we are like a cracked or dirty cup that can turn the precious liquid into poison.

When we start to follow a teaching, there are essential qualities we must have as practitioners. It is important to have a good master and to receive clear instructions, to have great respect for the master and the teachings, to develop the capacity to practice, and not to be like the wind but be stable in our practice and in ourselves.

Until we have confidence in our practice, we need many things: the opportunity to practice, the right posture, a comfortable seat, and self-control when we practice. But it is very important at the start not to push ourselves too hard, not to try straightaway to sit for marathon sessions but rather to engage in many short practice sessions and, as we become accustomed to engaging in sitting meditation, to increase the length of the periods of practice. Nor should we immediately think we need special, secret practices, but instead be content with the practices we are given, which are more suitable to our state of mind as beginning practitioners. We must heed whether what we have been taught is clear to us or not. If it is not, then we must practice to make the fundamental points clear, because if we have established a good foundation, we can consolidate the base and receive further teachings, otherwise it is pointless to seek further, secret teachings. If we cannot put into practice the basic teachings, the simplest ones, how can we expect to be able to practice the higher teachings? In this way, feeding our expectations would only make us regress. Nor should we ask ourselves (or the master), "When will I get realized?" The main point to bear in mind in relation to meditation is to avoid indulging in spiritual fantasies and to remember that the fundamental purpose of the practice is to acquire, maintain, and develop continuity of presence of awareness.

Starting Dzogchen Practice

When we start to practice, in order to grasp the normal mind, our first practice consists in engaging our mind. For example, if we have a problem of some kind, we may go to a movie to distract ourselves from our problem. Likewise when we start to practice, we try to calm down our problem-creating mind in order to be able to observe the nature of thought. The observation of the arising, abiding, and dissolving of thought in the empty state of the mind is an essential practice in Dzogchen in order to discover that moving thoughts are of the same nature as the thoughtless state of the mind. Since we are not accustomed to meditation, it seems very difficult, and every slight sound or movement, outside or inside the mind itself, becomes a major distraction interfering with our ability to continue to practice. In order to overcome this problem, we engage the mind in a practice so that it is not so easily distracted, by focusing attention so that the movement of the mind caused by thought or sense perception does not have the power to divert our concentration. This first stage, of grasping the mind, is concentration practice, described in detail in the Bonpo *Ati* system. It has three stages.

Engaging the Mind in Concentration Practice

The first stage of concentration involves fixation and requires some effort, as we are beginning to tame the mind and have not yet reached the calm state. When we have mastered the mind, the moment comes when the practice becomes natural for us; it no longer requires an effort on our part, just as learning something is always difficult at first but becomes easier with practice. The third and final stage is when we have the right experience and achieve the stage of relaxation, of "dissolved *zhiné*" in which we are able to remain in the state of concentrated attention without needing to expend any effort to avoid distraction. However, it is important not to confuse this relaxed state with the total relaxation of contemplation practice, when we effortlessly remain in the non-dual state of presence. Once we have applied to calm down our thoughts and have then applied insight meditation to observe the mind, the master confirms our experience of the natural mind gained through the latter practice.

Introduction in Dzogchen

In Dzogchen, the introduction to the natural state of the mind is of great importance because it is an introduction to the fundamental base within the individual. It is on this fundamental base (that is, the view of Dzogchen) that we must establish our practice and from which we must apply to our behavior in daily life in the correct way.

After we have received this introduction, it is important to have the experience ourselves, otherwise it is possible to develop many fantasies about it. Some people think "direct introduction" means sitting with a master and having some kind of feeling or experiencing a special atmosphere. They mistake this for understanding; but this kind of direct introduction does not last long. It is also important to identify what the explanations refer to in terms of our own direct experience. In fact, there is nothing spoken about in the teachings that we cannot find in ourselves, in our own experience. The problem I see is that often practitioners do not enter into direct experience of the real primordial condition but live in a concept, so that there is nothing real on which to base their practice and from which to develop. Without direct experience, the teachings become intellectual talk or a mere collection of new things to learn and will not make any real sense or effect any changes in our lives. Without the groundwork of *zhiné*, it is difficult to enter into the experience of emptiness and clarity and their inseparability, so that we are continually searching for new things to learn about Dzogchen and new practices to do; but once we have the experience, then we are satisfied with that and only need different skillful ways to develop it. Actually to reach that experience and understanding is the ultimate goal, and all that there really is left to do is to sit quietly; but many people are not satisfied with that.

Dealing with Mistakes and Obstacles

When we start to practice, it is important to distinguish fundamental from less significant mistakes. For example, if we do not know how to pronounce a mantra correctly or are not sure of the details or colors of a visualization, these are not fundamental mistakes. The principle and intention of our practice are more important than the details of sound or vision. But misunderstanding the pure state of mind is a fundamental mistake. How is it possible to make such a major mistake? By understanding in the wrong way from the very beginning or by starting with correct understanding but trying to force the practice with the result that we develop it in the wrong way.

It is of fundamental importance to identify the pure state of the mind unmistakably. The pure state of mind is the essence of the Sutras, of the Tantras, of Mahamudra, and of Dzogchen. In this context it is important to learn to distinguish between pure and impure states of presence. When we understand the difference between these two and apply this comprehension to our practice, visions and signs of spiritual progress arise more easily. These signs serve to enable us to continue practicing without effort and to remain in the state of contemplation once we have discovered it. Without understanding pure presence, it will be very difficult to succeed in swiftly developing our practice. For example, a practitioner who had practiced for eleven years without making any progress went to his master, who explained to him the correct way to distinguish practice done in the pure state from that done in the impure state. Following this elucidation, the practitioner was able to gain realization in two years.

It is also necessary to have intellectual understanding, but that is not sufficient in itself. We have to feel as well as understand everything perfectly and then put it into practice. Intellectual understanding alone can prove more of an obstacle than a help unless it is accompanied by direct experience gained through practice. Once we have understood all these aspects, we will be able to progress quickly.

Effort and commitment to practice are necessary. No obstacle that arises in *zhiné* practice, such as laziness or mental agitation, should divert us and no kind of daily activity should distract us. We must integrate the state of pure, non-dual mind, discovered and developed through contemplation, into every situation and every moment of ordinary daily life.

Developing Our Practice

In the "Introduction to the Profound Essence" in the *Zhang Zhung Nyan Gyud*, there is an explanation of the three basic stages in *tögel* practice (see Chapter 15) the practitioner must undertake after having completed the preliminary practices. These stages can usefully be applied to how we should develop practice in general. The first stage consists in grasping the mind. Here "mind" means the everyday mind. The second stage consists in remaining in the understanding of the underlying essence of the mind attained by having overcome the everyday mind. The third stage consists in clarifying and developing the inner awareness of the essence of the mind by remaining in contemplation.

However, before we achieve the ability to abide in the state of contemplation and integrate it with our whole life, we must first develop the strength of our meditation. When we start to meditate, it is best to alternate short sessions of formal practice with rest periods, gradually increasing the duration of the sessions as we become more accustomed to relaxing in the calm state of mind.

There are precise instructions that advise the beginning practitioner regarding what secondary causes are beneficial when first undertaking the path of meditation. As regards the place, it should be a calm place with positive energy and without obstacles created by spirits. Ideal places are islands, caves, mountains, and, generally speaking, any place where the air is pure and there is not too much noise. However, the most important thing is to develop the capacity to practice in our normal daily life, at home, and not to live in a meditation "fantasy cave" removed from everyday reality. We should try not to sit near fires, in the hot sun, or in places where it is very windy.

The best time to practice is when the air is clean, either during the day or night, preferably early in the morning, about six or seven o'clock, and in the evening. One should not practice near midnight or midday when we feel more tired. If we practice before going to bed and feel drowsy or sleepy, it is best to try to become more alert by moving a little and inhaling deeply. But if we do not manage to wake up in this way, it is best to go to bed, as to continue is fruitless and we will neither practice nor sleep properly. It is better not to practice with too many people, but rather with just one or two spiritual friends who can help and encourage us to develop our practice. We should not talk too much or indulge in idle gossip. We should eat moderately in order to balance the elements and avoid alcohol and foods that dull the senses and the mind. We should also try to avoid strenuous work and brusque movements like dancing or jumping.

As regards the mind, when we are about to begin, it is best not to make plans or conjectures but instead relax the mind from the start. Do not be like the people referred to in the Tibetan proverb that says, "When we are happy, we abide in happiness: we sing, laugh, and enjoy ourselves; but when we have some problems, we remember the teaching and the guru." Instead it is best to practice as much as possible when the mind is clear and without problems and when we are in good shape mentally and physically, because then we can have experiences and signs of progress. It is best to start to practice when young. At this time the channels are still supple, the *prana* is still fresh and clean, and we have not yet acquired hardened mental habits. If we start young, we will surely obtain knowledge of the primordial state and its styles of manifestation before we need that understanding at the moment of death.

However, although it is best to start to practice when we are young, there are many stories in the Dzogchen teachings of persons, like Pang Mipam Gompo, who started to practice very late in life but who managed to achieve enlightenment through application.

Obstacles to Practice

There are several types of distraction that can become hindrances to practice. They are categorized as outer, inner, and secret obstacles. Outer obstacles are persons such as friends or relatives in so far as they might cause diversions, disturbances from the atmosphere, or negative spirits that can disturb our mental equilibrium, and distraction caused by attachment to objects and possessions. Inner obstacles are illnesses, not feeling like doing anything, and not knowing what to do. Secret obstacles are obstacles that disturb our inner practice, such as mental problems that prevent it from developing in the right way. They are called "secret" not because they are mysterious but because they belong to our innermost being and because we do not speak about them. How to deal with these problems is discussed in a chapter in the *Zhang Zhung Nyan Gyud* called "Removing Obstacles."

Obstacles are also classified into three other main categories: those that emerge in the view, those that emerge in meditation, and those that emerge in behavior. For example, if we talk too much about the view, it can become the object of philosophical speculation and intellectual conceptualization. This can hinder us from entering into direct experience. Again, if we form opinions with inadequate knowledge, we will not be able to apply direct understanding since our inaccurate concepts will cause doubts to arise continuously. To be able to talk about the practice but not to be able to apply it in our life is the inner obstacle of the view. The effect of this obstacle is to cause us to postpone practice continuously, never going beyond the level of conceptual understanding.

The obstacles to meditation pertain to experiences that can arise and distract us during our meditation practice, preventing us from remaining in contemplation. For example, we might have a feeling of great joy, but if we get carried away by this experience and fail to integrate it with our meditation, this joy can become an obstacle since we might become attached to it. Certainly there is nothing wrong with relaxing and enjoying the pleasurable feelings, but we must not forget that this is not the purpose of meditation. Another obstacle to meditation is simply sitting without thoughts. This is a state of relaxation, not meditation. In fact, it is a type of ignorance and should not be mistaken for the state of presence, which is a state of the union of emptiness with clarity, that is, relaxation with awareness. It is important to understand what is meant by "presence" in Dzogchen with regard to contemplation practice. Moreover, when during contemplation the thought arises, "This is real practice, this is true contemplation!" this is merely another concept and a type of secret obstacle to meditation. Similarly, after a moment of direct understanding of emptiness by presence during the observation of thoughts, when the thought arises "Ah, this is emptiness!" it is likewise another concept and no longer real understanding through presence. Thought has started to arise again! We must distinguish carefully between the direct, conceptless understanding of emptiness, which is fundamental in Dzogchen, and the kind of conceptual understanding of emptiness achieved by thought in the Sutras, where presence lacks clarity.

The element type of the practitioner is also important in relation to the types of obstacles we are likely to encounter and in
relation to determining what are the best remedies to overcome
these. For those persons with a prevalence of earth or water elements (in terms of personality type, not astrological elements), it
will take longer for the signs to manifest, but once these have been
obtained, the practice will develop more swiftly. Just as these elements are more stable, so the signs indicate greater stability in the
practice. On the other hand, a person more of an airy or fiery type
will get the signs sooner but will develop them less quickly and
easily. At first contemplation may seem easier for this type, but
then problems may arise and it will be more difficult to develop
the practice. In general, this element type takes many teachings
but does not then practice them: it would be better to practice more
fixation.

It is necessary to overcome all these obstacles because, if we
have disturbing thoughts, these can stop us from doing certain
practices. So it is important to bear in mind all the possible obstacles that can arise and take steps to remove them. For example,
in the case of illness we can try to balance the inner elements by
taking medicine or by other means. In the case of the secret obstacles, it is important to enter and remain in the state of the inseparability of emptiness and clarity without distraction. The outer
obstacles are the easiest to overcome; the inner obstacles are a little
more difficult, but the hardest to overcome are the secret obstacles.
In any event, the ultimate way of dealing with problems is to understand that they are created by thoughts and are a manifestation of our inner condition. It is necessary to return to their original
source. Once we discover their origin through direct experience,
we realize that in the primordial state really there are no thoughts
and consequently no problems, that in reality no problems exist,
that problems are the creation of our own moving mind, and that
no problem is more important than understanding the unreal nature of problems.

A particularly dangerous obstacle can arise if, over the course
of our life, we receive many teachings. The obstacle arises if we
come to consider the teachings no longer important. We have heard
them so often that we begin to get bored. The first time we heard
them they aroused great faith and respect, but after receiving them

several times without putting them into practice, gradually we grow distant and finally give them up. We can avoid this obstacle by, when we receive a teaching, practicing it until we actualize it. In this way we will become established in the state of meditation, so that there is no longer the possibility of being overpowered or distracted by thoughts. Then the signs of progress will surely start to manifest. These signs are useful as indications that we are applying the practice in the right way. It is important, however, not to have expectations or make conjectures about these signs, either before or during their occurrence, as they themselves might then become an obstacle rather than a benefit. If the signs of progress become the object of attachment, then they are a worse "positive" obstacle than the "negative" obstacles we encounter when we first start to practice. Moreover, we may not get any signs and feel this means we are not progressing; we should not get stuck and suffer on account of this but instead persevere without forcing the practice or having expectations.

The Ultimate Aim of Practice

It is important that our practice bring a sense of meaning into our lives, otherwise we will continue to perform only meaningless, distracting activities, like trying to become richer or more intelligent than others or always trying to find new lovers. Most of us have spent so much time acting this way that by now we should be jaded, but it is difficult to escape from all this. By receiving teachings and practicing them, we can do something that can give a purpose to our lives. If we understand and have direct experience of our true condition, then at the end of our life we may even succeed in not encountering death. The culmination of the Dzogchen path is the attainment of the "rainbow body" where the adept passes on without leaving mortal remains. But even if we do experience and show the signs of physical death, our practice during our life will have helped us to prepare for it. We will die happily and confidently because we will have some idea of what will happen during the death process and after death in the intermediate *bardo* state, and we will be ready to face these experiences.

If we think Dzogchen is useful psychologically to help understand and resolve problems in this life, that is fine, but that is not its principal aim and we must not stop at that. All the practice we do in this life is useful not only for this life, but for a longer period, for our next life too. The ultimate aim of the practice is to achieve continuous presence in the primordial state, which is always luminous, and which is liberation itself.

6

Zhiné
Calm Abiding in Tranquility

I am the great self-arisen naturally-abiding one
Known from the beginning as the origin of all things.
You, strenuously seeking me and yearning for me,
Fatigue yourselves; even over many eons you do not
      find me.
This nature of mine is unique among all things,
Not comparable to what is not me or what tries to be
      me.

The Practice of Concentration

Concentration practices such as *zhiné* are found in many traditions, for example, Sutric and Tantric Buddhism and the many forms of Hinduism. In all these traditions, it is considered a necessary and fundamental practice. In Dzogchen, *zhiné* is considered a preparation for the essential practice of contemplation. In fact, it is very difficult to get very far in the practice of Dzogchen contemplation without first having practiced *zhiné*.

In Dzogchen, concentration practice has three stages. The first stage is "forced" concentration. It involves the application of effort and is sometimes called "the creation of the person." We persist in the practice to improve concentration because we are not accustomed to it. This is the phase of mind-created tranquillity. In the second stage, we develop this forced, effortful concentration until it transforms into a state of natural tranquillity. In the third stage, we relax the concentration until it turns into a state of stable tranquillity.

Engaging in concentration practice is very important because it is very difficult to reach understanding of the true state without it, and even if we do gain understanding, it is very difficult to sustain that understanding for any length of time unless we have developed sufficient power of concentration. Actually, the ability to concentrate is very important in all the spiritual paths, not only Dzogchen, and also in ordinary everyday life.

In Dzogchen, concentration is one of the fundamental preliminary practices. Through it we calm and gain control over the moving mind and, most importantly, through it we can be introduced by the master to "the natural state of the mind." It is also an important practice that experienced practitioners use to help them stabilize that state. In the Bon tradition, after completing the preliminary practices and receiving the initiation of Zhang Zhung Meri, the practitioner engages in the practice of *zhiné* under the guidance of an experienced master who introduces him to knowledge of the innate natural state of his mind. The *zhiné* practice delineated in this chapter comes from the *Ati* system of Bonpo Dzogchen.

Zhiné Practice from the Ati

Zhiné practice of the *Ati* system consists of two techniques of concentration practice. These are referred to as "fixation with an attribute" and "fixation without an attribute." In fixation practice with an attribute, a visible support, such as an image, is used to concentrate mental attention and bring the mind under control using effort. When this has been achieved and the practice has become more relaxed, we are introduced to the practice of the observation of the mind leading to insight into the natural state. We then proceed, under the master's guidance and instructions, to fixation without an attribute. This involves meditation on our unconditioned nature and consists of training in keeping the mind in the state of contemplative equipoise.

Teachings generally are given in a certain order: first, the preliminary practices, then fixation, introduction to the natural state, and, finally, contemplation. We are advised to practice them in that order because it is helpful, useful, and actually necessary to do it in this way. Otherwise, it is like wanting to do the third year at school after the first year without having done the second; without doing the second year not only will we not be able to do the third, we will not be able to go on to the fourth and fifth years. There is a certain order that has to be followed. This does not mean that there may not be certain people who have greater ability to develop their practice through fixation without an attribute and who do not get signs of progress when they do fixation with an attribute; but obviously this does not apply to everybody, so it is better to follow the traditional order and instructions.

The attribute is an object that serves as a mental "support" in order to concentrate the attention for the fixation practice. In the case of the *Ati* system, the attribute used as the point of focus of attention is the Tibetan letter *A*. This is used in order to eliminate all the thoughts that distract the mind. Although *A*, which is the last letter in the Tibetan alphabet and the base of all the other letters, is very rich in symbolic meaning (it symbolizes the pure state of the mind), in this practice its function is simply to focus the attention. In fact, any object, such as an image or a swastika, can be used.

There is a good reason for using a physical support for the fixation practice: it is easier than trying to create a fixation point mentally by visualization, which does not always work and is somewhat difficult.

Prepare a piece of indigo paper one inch square with the Tibetan letter *A* drawn as illustrated on page 89. The *A* should be enclosed in five concentric, colored circles. The central circle should be indigo. This should be surrounded by green, red, yellow, and white in that order. (If one feels uncomfortable with the Tibetan letter, an English "A" can be used in its place.) Place the paper on a stick high enough so that the square can rest about one and one half feet in front of your nose.

We should start with short periods of meditation practice alternated with brief off-meditation intervals. During the latter, we should not give in to distraction, but we should do practices such as the visualization of a deity or the generation of compassion. Gradually, as we become more accustomed to remaining in the state of concentration, we can extend the duration of the periods of practice.

The *Ati* instructions explain that the best time to practice is in the morning. As the mind is clearer when we wake up because during the night it does not elaborate conceptual thoughts, and the thinking process takes a little time to resume its normal activity. The instructions go on to elucidate the rules to be followed concerning body posture, breathing, gaze, mind, and attention. As regards the body, we should sit cross-legged with the right foot resting on the left leg, with the thumb touching the root of the ring finger (or "finger of the spirits," so called because it is through this finger that spirits enter a medium's body). The shoulders should be kept open and not hunched. The back must be straight and the stomach pulled in, with the chin slightly tucked into the throat. The breathing should be kept as natural as possible. Breathing too fast causes the attention to be disturbed. As regards the gaze, we must not look up or down but stare straight at the letter *A*. The eyes should not be wide open, otherwise the mind may grasp the *A* as an external object, or closed, otherwise we may start to doze and fall into a sleepy state. We must not blink the eyes or inhibit the flowing of "the three waters": saliva from the mouth, mucus from the nose, and tears from the eyes. These must be allowed to flow freely, because we must concentrate and not allow these reflex actions to distract us. As regards the attention, the *Ati* explains that we should concentrate as if we were putting a thread into the eye of a needle. As regards the mind, we should neither think of the past nor the future, nor should we try to change the present situation. We must simply maintain presence of awareness of the *A*, but without thinking about the *A*, and concentrate as intensely as possible. We must not lose awareness of the *A* even for a second.

It is important to distinguish between simply maintaining presence of awareness of the *A*, that is, directing the attention continuously to the *A* without the stream of attention being distracted, and actively thinking about the *A*, which is merely creating another thought. In fact, there are two stages of looking at the *A*: the initial stage is when we concentrate, which means using the *A* to control thoughts and the mind. The second stage is when we are absorbed in contemplation and are merely aware that there is an *A* without any no longer concentrating attention on the *A*.

By following these rules strictly, we harmonize and put into action the internal elements, our practice starts to work, and our mind comes under control. The mind follows the eyes: when a person looks, the mind passes through the eyes. If we gaze at the *A* but our mind wanders somewhere else, this is not concentration on the *A*.

Dealing with Problems

At first it may be difficult to concentrate properly. The effort involved can give rise to problems. The eyes burn, the body wants to move, and we may decide we don't like practicing in this way. This also depends on our element type as we have seen, as well as our general way of being, and at the start we must make an effort to control this. For example, there are people who are more agitated than others and always need someone to talk to: it is good for this type of person to start with fixation practice with the *A* in order to change this personality trait a little.

If, during the practice, we think about what we are doing, or should be doing, this is distraction by thought and not concentration. Likewise, if we pay attention to the comfort of the posture, this is not concentration either. If we are truly concentrated, we do not notice the comfort or discomfort of the body or even the flowing of "the three waters."

If we do not attain understanding through fixation on the *A*, we should try practicing fixation with advanced practitioners, or practicing with sound, using a neutral sound such as *HUM*. For example, we can sit with other practitioners and pronounce the sound 100 to 1000 times, trying to concentrate on the sound as much as possible. (Practice with sound is also very useful for blind practitioners, who are physically unable to concentrate on a visual image, and also for elderly people who are not very active physically and mentally.) If even then we do not succeed, we should start again, going on a pilgrimage to sacred places or receiving an initiation and repeating the preliminary practices, and then resuming the fixation practice. Thereby, in time, we will certainly gain understanding.

Signs of Spiritual Progress

According to the *Ati* system, there are signs of spiritual progress, grouped into different kinds of internal and external signs, that will indicate that we have gained a certain amount of control over our mind. It is important to get these signs, but it is also important not to seek to obtain them. In fact, in knowing the signs beforehand there is the risk that we may willfully create them.

It is possible to get one sign, some signs, or all the signs together. If there are no signs, we must intensify our practice using sound until we begin to get them. There are eight internal signs, each with an illustrative example.

The first sign is like a turtle that, when put in a basin of water, retracts its limbs into its shell. The practitioner feels almost as if her mind cannot move. This is a sign of the mind turning inwards.

The image for the second sign is a little bird in a cold wind that starts to tremble. Our mind starts to tremble because it is becoming very subtle and clear.

The third sign is the disordered way that crabs thrown onto a table move, or the random way grapes thrown onto a table come to rest, each grape in its own position. This is a sign that the mind is not restrained or involved in making judgments but has effortlessly assumed the natural condition. This means that after a meditation session, we are in a natural and relaxed state without there being any forced or imposed order in our thoughts; it is a loose relaxed state, the opposite of the first sign of turning inwards.

The example for the fourth sign is derived from ancient times, before there were matches and Tibetans still used to strike a flint against a tinder box to light a fire. Sometimes you get a spark, sometimes you don't. This means that in the meditation session we feel that sometimes we are in a calm state and sometimes we are not. It also means that sometimes we have understanding and sometimes we do not. By having both experiences, we can comprehend what is true understanding and identify when we are in the calm state.

The fifth sign is like water flowing through a very narrow tube or tap. This means that the state of mind has become stable and very subtle and even and that there is a continuous fine flow.

The sixth sign is like a bee that does not want to move far from a flower full of nectar. This means we feel very good during concentration practice; we have attachment to that happiness and do not want to stop. However, this is not a negative kind of attachment but a desire to continue to practice, a desire not to stop. This means the practice is working since we feel comfortable and can continue practicing for a long time.

The seventh sign is like a fish swimming or jumping in the sea in any direction it likes, without being concerned about possible obstacles or accidents. This is like a sudden sensation of freedom, a feeling that in whichever direction the mind moves, whatever thought arises in the mind, there is no disturbance or distraction.

The eighth sign is like the wind blowing through tree leaves in autumn without getting stuck to anything. This means that whatever thoughts arise the mind continues to flow without forming attachments.

There are also external signs that serve as indications of progress. The first of these, as in the sixth sign above, is not wishing to move, but the movement here is more physical than mental. Whereas, in the internal sign, it was the mind that did not wish to move, in this case, it is the body. When I learned this fixation practice, I was with two other people, a monk and his sixty-five year old mother. When we finished the practice session, our master chanted for half an hour, after which the old lady could not move: that was the first sign she received.

Other signs are wishing to laugh or to cry for no apparent reason, or wanting to jump, or the complexion of our face changing color, or our body starting to tremble, or not wanting to continue sitting. Actually there is no limit to the kinds of signs we can get. It may seem like we are going a little crazy, but there is nothing wrong with this. It is just that we are undergoing internal changes and that our internal energy is being harmonized. These are all signs that we have captured the mind.

The *Zhang Zhung Nyan Gyud* gives another series of signs of progress using three examples. The text says it takes at least ten to fourteen days of practice to experience these signs of achieving a calm state of mind. The first example, which applies to the superior practitioner whose mind is without grasping, is of putting a turtle in a vase: the turtle has nothing to do so it is in a state without thoughts. This is a sign of entering into oneself. The second example applies to the average practitioner's experience and is of sending water through a pipe: this is a sign that the flow of the mind is straight and direct, not wavering or distracted by thoughts. The third example applies to the inferior practitioner and is of a bee stopping as long as possible at a flower to take nectar: this is a sign that the mind is relaxed and joyful and without the movement of thoughts but still is grasping: it wants to remain in the calm state.

All these signs produce a certain effect because they enable us to practice without effort, and this is important because they stimulate us to continue for longer sessions without strain.

Introduction to the Natural State

When the inner and outer signs start to manifest, the master introduces us to the natural state by explaining to us the nature of the experiences we have already had and of the knowledge we have already acquired by ourselves. In this way the practice becomes more calm and relaxed, less fixation and concentration practice and more like contemplation practice.

It is at this stage, when we have gone beneath the surface of the moving mind, that the master asks us about our experience of the natural state of the mind. The questions are about the nature of the mind: whether it has shape or color or a precise location; and then about the origin and nature of thought: whence thought arises, where it abides, where it dissolves, and who observes the thought. He might ask, "Who are you?", or "What is your mind? Has it got a color or a form?" or "Where do your thoughts come from?" but without ever suggesting the answer. Only when we have gained understanding through the practice of insight into the mind and through our own immediate experience does the master show us the nature of the mind by directly pointing out to us our own ex-periential knowledge, explaining about the *kunzhi* and *rigpa* and their inseparability in the primordial state. In this way our under-standing will be clear and real since what the master explains and clarifies is knowledge we have gained for ourselves through our own direct experience. The master does not introduce his own con-cept, something we have not experienced ourselves, as this would produce merely intellectual understanding. He is introducing what we have already found within ourselves.

It is necessary to have this direct experience ourselves, and the surest way to do this is by practicing *zhiné*. Otherwise it is very easy to have intellectual fantasies about the nature of the primor-dial state, about "emptiness", "clarity", "light", "bliss," and so forth. When the primordial state is introduced through *zhiné*, we understand it thoroughly and are able to enter and remain in the state of contemplation. This is *trekchö* (see Chapter 15), one of the two main practices in Dzogchen.

Once we have gained control of the flux of thoughts in the mind through fixation with an attribute, the master introduces to us and guides us in the practice of fixation without an attribute. By the application of insight, we understand the movements of the thought-producing level of mind and so come to know the under-lying natural state of the mind. It has two stages.

The first consists in training by following four fundamental prin-ciples relating to body posture, gaze, gaining control of the mind, and the "commitment." Commitment (*samaya* in Sanskrit and *dam tshig* in Tibetan) generally refers to the vows undertaken when re-ceiving Tantric initiations and instructions; here it refers simply to the rules of body posture and so forth to be followed in this specific practice. The second consists in training to develop the practice.

Here the instructions concerning the body posture and the gaze are a little different from those previously given for fixation prac-tice with an attribute, as once we have gained control of the mind and understood "the state" we can relax more. There is no longer a need to make an effort to control thoughts since these are no longer an obstacle. At first the practice sessions need not be so long and strict; although, as in the case of fixation practice with an attribute, in general it is good to start with short sessions and then gradually to lengthen them so that the practice sessions become longer and the intervals shorter. It is better not to do physical activities that are too strenuous before a session as this will make the mind less stable and cause more thoughts to arise. We should try to avoid dancing, jumping, making brusque movements, and also talking needlessly and gossiping. As regards the mind, when about to begin practicing it is better not to make plans or think about things but to relax it right from the start.

If we have difficulty in starting contemplation and then later proceed well, that is good. What we have to do upon receiving a teaching is to practice it thoroughly and well, until we obtain the fruit of the practice; then, when we receive another teaching, practice that one properly in the same way. For example, if we receive instruction on fixation practice but do not practice it sufficiently and in the right way because we are anxious to receive higher teachings on contemplation, then, when we do practice contemplation, we will not be able to develop it properly because we have not completed the preliminary work.

Through the correct and thorough application of fixation, we can proceed from the first stage of forced concentration in which effort is required, through the stage of natural concentration in which practice is more relaxed and no longer requires such effort, to the final stage of stable concentration.

Once the master's introduction has clarified our understanding of the natural state, thoughts, which continue to arise, are no longer an obstacle, and there is the self-liberation of thoughts. In fact, by their nature thoughts are not an obstacle or a problem; they are a manifestation of the natural state. Thoughts arise from the natural state, abide in the natural state, and return to the natural state. If we do not allow thoughts to distract us by following after them or trying to suppress them, then we do not create attachment or aversion to them and they self-liberate in the natural state. We see thoughts as ornaments of the natural state.

Understanding can be of two types: with thought, which is conceptual, intellectual understanding; and without thought, which is direct understanding. Thoughts cannot be liberated by other thoughts: "good" thoughts cannot liberate "bad" thoughts, just as blood cannot wash away blood from a hand. "Good" and "bad" thoughts are both obstacles to direct understanding of the natural state, which is beyond thought, and thought cannot understand what is beyond thought. Understanding of the natural state can only be direct understanding not mediated by thought; it is the empty nature of the mind understanding itself.

Even when we have gained this direct understanding through presence, if the thought arises, "Ah, that is emptiness, now I understand," this is no longer direct understanding since we are distracted by that thought, which reduces direct understanding to conceptual understanding. The presence that understands emptiness is innate self-awareness. It is called innate self-awareness because it is the empty state understanding itself by its own clarity. Emptiness is not separate from clarity; the emptiness is the clarity and the clarity is the emptiness.

The practice of concentration is not yet contemplation, but through the development of concentration we can know the natural state and acquire the capacity to remain in the state of presence; that is the introduction to the practice of contemplation.

The Tibetan letter A

7

Nyamshag
Contemplation

When everything is realized as Buddha
Meditation and the view do not exist apart.
This very meditation is the superior view.

Buddha is neither found in meditation
Nor lost in lacking meditation.
Continuously remain in non-distraction.

The Meaning of Contemplation in Dzogchen

In Dzogchen, *nyamshag*, contemplation, has a precise and specific
meaning. It indicates presence in the state of the inseparability of
clarity and emptiness. In the symbolic language of Dzogchen, this
is the "union of mother and son." Contemplation is the foremost
Dzogchen practice.

The practices of meditation on emptiness performed on the Sutric
path and the practices of the Tantric path, such as the recitation of

mantras and the visualization of deities in order to obtain the unification of emptiness and bliss, are all secondary practices in Dzogchen, to be used when they are necessary. What we must develop as Dzogchen practitioners is the contemplation of the inseparability of emptiness and clarity in the natural state of mind. As these are already inseparable, in Dzogchen we do not try to unite them, as Tantric practitioners do, but simply to recognize their indivisibility. Secondary practices are only skillful means towards this development.

Concentration and Contemplation

It is important to understand the differences between concentration and contemplation. After having tamed the mind by engagement in fixation with an object and having achieved relaxed concentration through fixation without an object, we are ready for introduction to the state of contemplation and instructions on how to remain in the natural state. In concentration practice there is still dualism between the subject that is concentrating (fixing on the object) and the object of concentration (the object fixed on), and there still also remains dualism between inside (the consciousness inside the mind-body of the meditator) and outside (the object of meditation). But in contemplation there is no subject or object; it is said to be like "pouring water into water." In the Sutra system, on the third path of seeing, the inseparability of *nyamshag* (contemplation) and the post-meditation state is also compared to "pouring water into water." Here there is no longer relative existence, and perception is by yogic, direct perception. But according to Dzogchen, this level of experience is immediately attainable by the practitioner without having to wait to attain the path of seeing. Simply remaining in the state of contemplation where there is no inner or outer, where there is the recognition that all "outer" reality is a projection of the "inner" state, is sufficient.

Mind and Contemplation

It is important in Dzogchen to understand what type of mind remains in the state of contemplation. The Sutra (Chittamatra) tradition classifies types of mind as "direct" and "non-direct" perceivers. Direct perception, which is defined as non-conceptual, can be of four types: through the senses, mental, self-knowing, and yogic. According to Dzogchen, the kind of mind involved in contemplation is a direct perceiver but is not subsumed under any of the four classifications of the Sutra system. Although, according to Dzogchen, the consciousness that perceives the natural state is called "self-knowing," this does not correspond to the self-knowing direct perceiver of the Chittamatra system. In Dzogchen, "self" is connected with emptiness, the unfabricated base of everything, also referred to as "*kunzhi.*" What is here translated as "knowing" (*rig*), more precisely means the awareness of that base together with emptiness and its non-dual manifestation as energy. "Self-knowing" in Dzogchen thus means being aware of the single totality of the base of everything in one's own being, as opposed to being aware of each aspect of consciousness, part by part. "Self-knowing" in Chittamatra, on the contrary, does not refer to emptiness but is a possibility for each kind of consciousness; that is, each consciousness has its own "self-knowing," namely, that aspect of its own constitution that is aware of itself. For instance, a particular, momentary eye-consciousness of an apple has its own self-knowing, namely, that aspect of the awareness of the apple that is also conscious of itself. In Dzogchen, this understanding is completely beyond conceptual mind, which is incapable of direct understanding. The way of understanding is direct and the way of remaining in the state of contemplation is without distinction of knower and known, subject and object. This mind, which is beyond any conceptual mind and which understands the natural primordial state, is a subtle inner mind also known as the "clear light," where (in the terminology of the dream practice) "clear" refers to the emptiness and "light" refers to the clarity of the primordial mind.

Mind and the Nature of Mind

It is also important to differentiate between the nature of the mind or "mind as such" (*sems nyid*, synonymous in Bon Dzogchen thought with *kunzhi*, the "ground of everything") and the mind (*sems*). In the *Zhang Zhung Nyan Gyud* there is a classification of four qualities that differentiate the nature of the mind from the mind.

The four qualities of the nature of the mind are:

1. absence of thoughts;
2. being the basis of the moving mind;
3. being neutral, without the bias of being virtuous or nonvirtuous;
4. having unlimited potentiality for manifestation.

The four qualities of the mind are:

1. seeing and memory;
2. that when the mind thinks, any thought can manifest;
3. that when one does not think and observes the moving mind, it liberates into *kunzhi*;
4. that if one allows one's mind to abide in the unchanging natural state, the mother and the son join inseparably (see Chapters 10 and 11 below).

According to the Sutric Chittamatra, the mind is analyzed as having three qualities: *sem* (*sems*), *yi* (*yid*) and *lo* (*blo*). *Lo* is "a strong subjective tendency" while *sem* is "mental attitude" and *yi* is the rational mind. However, according to the *Zhang Zhung Nyan Gyud*, *sem* (discursive mind), *lo* (intellect) and *yi* (conceptual mind) are basically the same.

Methods of Contemplation

The *Zhang Zhung Nyan Gyud* lists nine methods to acquire the experience of contemplation:

1. To remove distractions by the threefold control of the actions of the body, speech, and mind;
2. To find oneself in the natural state of mind by three deliverances: releasing the body into the state of physical inaction, speech into silence, and mind into absence of thought;
3. To abide in awareness (*rig pa*) by a threefold method of remaining: remaining in the mind as such as it is by not changing the moving mind; remaining in the essence of the natural condition, remaining without limitation in the natural state.

4. To interrupt the continuation of the karmic traces with respect to the three actions: not following after the actions of the body, not following after words, not following after the desires of the mind.

5. To prolong abiding in the natural state with the three strengths: reinforcing the strength of undistracted presence, which is awareness itself; reinforcing the strength of the unconditioned self; reinforcing the natural strength of uninterrupted blissfulness.

6. To protect the knowledge acquired by a threefold hiding: hiding the body from disturbances like game animals hiding from hunters; hiding words in great silence like concealing a butter lamp in a vessel; hiding the moving mind in the nature of mind from the six sense objects, like a turtle hiding in the ocean.

7. To train the energy of awareness by the three appearances: the appearance of the various actions of the body arising in the actionless state of the body; the appearance of the various arisings of speech in silence; the appearance of the various movements of the moving mind in the thoughtless state. With these three one sees all appearances as equal, because their source is the absence of the three actions.

8. To find the non-dual state by the three liberations: all the actions of the body liberate in the actionless state of the body; all speech liberates in silence; all thoughts liberate in the thoughtless state of the mind. By these liberations we understand the fundamental underlying equality of the mind and the nature of the mind.

9. To obtain the final result by the three non-obscurations: actions do not obscure the actionless state of the body; speech does not obscure silence; thoughts do not obscure the thoughtless state. By achieving the final non-obscuration, the ultimate result manifests.

Thoughts and Contemplation

One's relationship to the arising of thoughts is a crucial aspect of contemplation. Through observation of the arising, remaining, and dissolving of thought in emptiness, we perceive the true, empty nature of thought: thoughts are the movement of the mind and are of the same nature as the natural mind, just as waves are of the same watery nature as the sea. When thoughts arise during the state of contemplation, we are aware that they arise from emptiness and that their essence is of the nature of emptiness. We are not disturbed by them but let them go, remaining in the equanimity of contemplation. In this way the natural state of emptiness becomes clearer: we encounter the union and the identity of clarity (*rig pa*) and emptiness (*kun gzhi*) directly in our own experience, so that we can then realize the inseparability of clarity and emptiness in the natural state. What is important for us is to reach the condition in which we are no longer distracted or disturbed by thoughts. This is not a blank state in which thoughts are absent. In fact, the cultivation of the calm state without thoughts, if prolonged beyond the natural gap that exists between two thoughts, becomes a state of ignorance, not of presence, if in the forced absence of thoughts there is only emptiness without clarity, relaxation without presence. In the true state of contemplation we are relaxed and neither create nor block thoughts but remain present without distraction in the mind-moments of both presence and absence of thoughts. Dzogchen contemplation is presence in the state beyond thoughts because the conceptual, thought-creating mind, which is accustomed to keeping the mind's attention by its continuous production of thoughts, is at rest. The conceptual, thought-creating mind pushes the practitioner away from the relaxed state of contemplation into tension. This makes it difficult to remain relaxed in the state of contemplation for any length of time.

Three Types of Experience in Contemplation

In this presence there are three types of experience (*nyams*): the experience of bliss (*bde ba'i nyams*), a sensation of inner pleasure; the experience of emptiness (*stong pa'i nyams*), a sensation of total dissolution in space, wherein nothing exists; and the experience of clarity (*gsal ba'i nyams*), a sensation of extreme lucidity, in which there is direct understanding by presence without the mediation of thought. However, these three *nyams* must not be confused with rigpa or with the primordial state. They are experiences that are comprehended by *rigpa*, the self-awareness of the state.

Presence in Dzogchen

Presence has a particular meaning in Dzogchen. "Presence" is a word that can be applied to anything in general: anything can be "present." In everyday life presence can refer to careful attention in daily activities or work, if we draw a bow to shoot an arrow, there is presence in the energy released by the bow and by ourselves in shooting the arrow at the target. In terms of spiritual practice there are different types of presence: presence in energy, presence in power, presence in joy, and presence in clarity; but when we talk about presence in the context of Dzogchen it specifically indicates being present in the inseparability of clarity and emptiness in the natural state of the mind.

Likewise, there is a great difference between the ordinary meaning of distraction, which in everyday speech refers simply to diversion of attention, and the import it has in Dzogchen, where it refers to absence from the natural state.

Sometimes, for example if we cut our finger in the kitchen, we might hear someone say, "You are a Dzogchen practitioner, how can you get distracted while you are cooking?" But that is not the principle. As Dzogchen practitioners, it is possible to get distracted while cooking, but not possible to get distracted from the natural state.

For example, think of winning a lot of money in a lottery. We would be very happy, and if, when we went home, we found a broken window, we might suffer for that but at the same time we would be happy because we would remember and still "be present" to having won the lottery. Our neighbour, who hasn't won the lottery, might also have a broken window, so we would have the same problem, but in different ways. When we are present, we suffer just as all people suffer, but our way of suffering is different and the result is different, because although we have problems and suffering, these cannot distract us from presence in the natural state; we are able to be present in any condition, so we relate every situation to practice.

According to Dzogchen, the five sense consciousnesses and the mental consciousness are very important. Let us examine presence in relation to these six consciousnesses once again by taking the example of going to the cinema. The senses are capable of non-conceptual cognition. When we are in the cinema, it does not matter whether the film is good or bad; our eyes see the film and our ears listen to the sound, the senses perceive the movements of form and sound and the perception is not blocked by mental judgment; our body is sitting in a comfortable seat; if it's summer, there will be air conditioning; if it is winter, there will be heating; our nose smells some nice perfume, and our tongue tastes some chocolate. All our senses work at the same time and never distract each other, nor do the sense perceptions give rise to thought. If we eat chocolate, it does not distract our eyes from seeing the film or our ears from hearing the soundtrack. The sense consciousnesses have this capacity because they experience directly without concepts; they are thoughtless so they can function together without interfering with each other. Our mental consciousness is comfortable because it is not judging. In that moment the mental functions are perceiving the forms of the film that are the objects of the sense consciousnesses and are not distracted by the intellect forming thoughts. Only when the film finishes do we start to perceive in a different way, because our mental consciousness starts to elaborate thoughts: we start to think and judge the film. At the cinema we use all the sense consciousnesses, but we are not in the state of presence. When we practice, all the sense consciousnesses function in the same way, but there is also self-presence.

This example is useful because when we are practicing, our sense consciousnesses work without distraction and we are present in the pure state of mind at the same time; we have self-awareness of emptiness not as a subject experiencing an object but as presence in the experience of self-awareness undistracted by conceptual thought. When we integrate with self-awareness and we have remained in that state for half an hour or more, depending on our capacity as practitioners, then we say we have finished: this is analogous to the end of the film. But in the cinema we experience the form of the sense object but not the emptiness of the sense object: we are not experiencing the natural quality inside the form, which is empty. Beyond the mind that perceives form, the object is empty, and it is this union of form and emptiness that we understand by applying the mind beyond concepts in contemplation.

As Dzogchen practitioners it is very important to work with presence, to develop it well and then to integrate it with our actions of body, voice, and mind in order to have total presence. But what is "total presence"? It is the continuity of presence. By practicing and reflecting on the examples, it is possible to understand total presence by direct experience.

Clarity in Contemplation

There is also a distinction drawn in the Bon teachings between ordinary contemplation and contemplation with clarity. Contemplation with clarity is accomplished by performing the purification practice of dissolving the *tiglé* (*thig le*), the visualized form of *rigpa* that is the clarity of the mind, in space, which is the emptiness of the mind, thus uniting emptiness and clarity. In that moment, if we are able to be present in clarity, we can develop it further.

In contemplation, there is direct, conceptless understanding through clarity. This kind of immediate understanding, which does not rely on the movement of thought, can know many things that generally go beyond the comprehension of the ordinary mind. It is without concepts because it arises directly from the empty nature of the mind, from the primordial state that is beyond thought.

Through contemplation we can have a transient experience of the individual condition of the natural primordial state that is always clear, luminous, and perfect, like the sun that always shines in the sky but can be temporarily obscured by clouds. It is we practitioners who have moments of clarity when we are present in the natural state, and moments of distraction when we are absent.

When we see with our eyes in the state of contemplation what we are really seeing is our own wisdom. The eyes are the portals of wisdom according to Bon Dzogchen. In the hermetic language of the *Zhang Zhung Nyan Gyud*, there is a great mountain in which there are five hermits and two caves. The great mountain is the body, the five hermits are the five wisdoms and the two caves are the eyes.

8

Integration

In the mind of Samantabhadra,
Experience called "present" or "absent" is erroneous.
That one excludes not the other is the ultimate
  excellence,
Clarified without effort, neither ascertained nor
  conceived.

The Importance of Integration

Great importance is given in Dzogchen to the integration of the
state of presence, developed through *zhiné* and then strengthened
through contemplation, with all the activities of body, voice, and
mind in daily life.

The Dzogchen practice of sky gazing (*nam mkhar gtad*) enables
us to integrate the empty condition of our mind with the empty
space of the sky, overcoming attachment to the ego and to the subtle
dualisms of inner and outer, and existence and nonexistence. But
before we can integrate our contemplation with the space that is

INTEGRATION

PRACTITIONER	VIEW	STATE	WAY OF LIBERATION	EXAMPLE
superior	absolute	continuity in state of contemplation	self-arising, self-liberation of the passions effortless and simultaneous	snowflakes dissolving in the ocean
average	meditation	application of wisdom of meditation in post-meditation periods	observation and recognition of the passions to liberate them some effort	sunbeams melting frost
inferior	mindfulness	application of attentive conceptual awareness to actions	recognizing passions and not following them application of mindful effort	hitting the target immediately

the true, absolute condition of the natural mind, we must be able to integrate with our thoughts and passions that are the condition of our relative mind. According to the *Zhang Zhung Nyan Gyud*, once we have stabilized our contemplation, it is important not only to remain in tranquility but also to "practice with the movements of energy of secondary causes." These are the energies of this present life, those that arise during the death process, and those that arise after death in the intermediate (*bar do*) state.

The secondary causes we have to work with in this present life fall into four main categories: those related to our existence in terms of body, voice, and mind; those related to the six sense consciousnesses (the five senses and the mind); those related to thoughts; and those related to our own various problems and limitations. We can prepare ourselves for experiences we will have during and after death by practicing in this life, and the way to turn our whole life into practice is to integrate contemplation with all our daily life activities. In order to do this, it is important to be very clear about what the state of contemplation is and how to remain in that state. In our practice it is important to try to remain in the state of presence and overcome the subtle dualistic division between contemplation and everyday life, between *thun* and *je thob*, between formal practice sessions and "after practice," and to integrate presence and contemplation with daily life.

This integration is very important in Dzogchen. If we compare the time we spend in formal practice with the amount of time we pass not practicing, it is easy to understand that if we limit our practice to formal meditation sessions without integrating our practice in all the activities of our daily life, it will take very many formal sessions to gain realization.

Integrating contemplation with daily life turns our whole life into practice and can lead to the attainment of realization in one single lifetime. Integration means the coordination of presence with the movement of energy and consists of the application of the pure wisdom of contemplation to our senses, to our body, voice, mind, and actions in every moment of our life by remaining present in the primordial state and imbuing all the activities of body, voice, and mind in daily life with awareness.

Integrating Presence with Actions

The way to do this is explained in great detail in the Bonpo *Ati* system of Dzogchen meditation, where the disciple is told to integrate first with virtuous actions, then neutral actions and finally nonvirtuous actions. In this way one makes all activities expressions of contemplative awareness; they become aids to spiritual development and so virtuous in the true sense.

In general, all actions, or movements of energy of our body, speech, and mind are considered as being virtuous, neutral, or nonvirtuous. Virtuous actions are those that do not distract us from the state of presence and that accumulate merit; nonvirtuous actions are those motivated by the five passions and that accumulate obstacles to spiritual development; neutral actions are those that have no karmic consequences and thus accumulate neither merit nor obstacles. Again, virtuous actions can be classified as absolutely virtuous and relatively virtuous. For example, in the case of the body, absolute virtue means remaining in the state of presence, while relative virtue refers to meritorious activities such as doing prostrations and circumambulating stupas, actions that generate benefit for oneself and for others.

Initially we try to integrate the state of contemplation with activities of the body, which are easiest, then with activities of speech, and finally with activities of the mind, which are the most difficult.

It is best to start with simple physical movements; for example, at the end of a session of meditation practice, while still in the state of presence, we might try to move our hand or arm, or to move an object like a cup, and see if we manage to remain in the state of contemplation during that movement: we must try to maintain the same condition of presence in the movement as in the calm, relaxed state. We can try to practice in this way for a week or so, training in making small, slow movements, until we notice that these slight movements are no longer a cause of distraction. Then we can see if we can integrate presence with greater movements: we can try to stand up while maintaining presence, then integrate presence with the act of walking. Next we can try to integrate with a virtuous activity such as performing prostrations, an activity that is slow and calm. Once we realize that these activities do not distract us from the state of presence, then we can try more energetic virtuous movements, for example, circumambulating stupas. Then, once we have integrated with virtuous actions such as these, we can attempt to integrate the state of presence with neutral actions: for example, eating slowly, with awareness. Once we can integrate with slow movements, we can try to integrate with faster movements such as running, jumping, swimming, and dancing. But first it is necessary to do all the preceding work, otherwise just going dancing in a disco, thinking we are remaining in presence when in fact we are completely distracted, is meaningless and can even be harmful.

When we notice we can integrate with these neutral movements, we must turn to nonvirtuous actions such as expressing the passion of anger; for example, hitting an animal. We try to integrate presence with this type of action. If we are able to integrate all these kinds of actions, this makes every single action of our body pure and virtuous because it is governed by presence.

The same applies to the voice. At first we should try to integrate the state of presence with the virtuous activities of the voice we normally perform after a practice session such as reciting mantras and chanting. When we notice these do not distract us, we can try to integrate with neutral activities such as singing ordinary songs or having ordinary conversations. Once we have integrated these, we can try to integrate with the four negative actions. These are: telling lies, slandering people to break friendships, insulting and quarreling with people, and gossiping. Some of these are easier to integrate than others, so we should start with those that are easier and less harmful, such as gossiping. Starting with quarreling and insulting would be more difficult as these cause an immediate reaction from the other person involved. But we must not stop at this point.

Many Westerners are disturbed by the idea that we practice integration with negative states, worrying that we seem to be justifying the harm our negativity does to others by merely changing our inner state rather than really doing something about the wrongs we commit by working to prevent them or compensating for them. But the point of integrating with negative states is not to justify wrong action. It is, rather, the best way to minimize harm and, ultimately, to overcome negativity. If we all mastered the practice of integration, there would be no harm or injury since we would all be in the non-dual state and when we are in the non-dual state we cannot cause harm.

It is also important to integrate presence with external sounds. When we start to practice *zhiné*, even sounds like bird songs and children's cries can distract us, but once we have developed our practice, these can no longer draw us away from presence. Now we can try to integrate presence with the sounds around us.

Finally, we should try to apply presence to the activities of the mind. Again, we should start with virtuous activities, such as doing guru yoga, purification, and Tantric visualization and transformation, and see whether these movements of the mind can distract us from contemplation. Once we are aware that we remain in the state of presence, we can experiment integrating neutral actions such as thinking of going out for a walk or calling someone to arrange to do something. Finally, we pass to nonvirtuous actions, for example, getting angry with someone. The principal nonvirtuous mental actions are those called the five poisons. These are: attachment to people and to things; anger, which can manifest when simply seeing someone gives rise to an unpleasant sensation; pride, which can manifest not only by thinking oneself to be very important but also by thinking one is the worst kind of person; jealousy, which means all kinds of comparisons and competition; and ignorance, which means not understanding the real condition. So in relation to the mind we start by trying to integrate with virtuous actions, then gradually pass to neutral actions, and finally to the five poisons. In this way, the whole mind, all thoughts — good, bad, and neutral — are integrated with the state of presence.

However, it is important to ascertain that we really do integrate presence with actions and do not simply think we are present while, in fact, we are distracted by actions. We must be aware that there is continuity of presence. This awareness that makes sure there is continuity of presence is like a secret helper who checks whether or not there is presence. It is called *dren shé* (*dran shes*) and is a kind of mindfulness.

Concerning integration with the movements of the mind; according to the *Zhang Zhung Nyan Gyud* there are 84,000 thoughts or movements of the mind every day; however, it is not the number of thoughts that arise that is important, but how we deal with them. There is actually only one way to deal with them, and that is not to be distracted by them. This can be done in three ways: by remaining in presence; by not following after them or creating more thoughts (such as the thought not to follow them); and by not allowing them to influence us (in this case it is not a matter of not following the thoughts but of not allowing the thoughts themselves to lead us away). In this way, all our 84,000 movements of thought, whether gross or subtle, and our passions are no longer like an ordinary person's; they are different in quality and serve for our practice.

So far we have talked about integrating presence with the body, voice, mind, and actions, in all the various aspects, virtuous, neutral and, nonvirtuous. What then is left? There are emotional states, such as shyness or sadness. For example, when we feel shy we can try to integrate completely with this condition and so discover there is no real shyness. Then there are the moments when we feel unhappy: it is also important to integrate this condition. If we can integrate with sadness, entering into it completely, we discover there is no sadness: if we can keep awareness in sadness, this helps very much in ordinary life situations as well as helping our practice. However, it is important to bear in mind that merely overcoming states of sadness is not the purpose of practice.

Of great importance for our practice is the state of startled awareness called *hedewa*. We can have moments of such awareness in daily life if someone nearby shouts suddenly, or when we vomit. These moments of startled awareness are very important for our practice. When these things happen in normal life, we do not usually manage to maintain self-awareness, but for our practice it is very important to remain in the state of presence and awareness in these situations, because they momentarily cut through the layer of conceptual mind and reveal a fresher state of consciousness.

Integrating Presence with Circumstances and Passions

We must be capable of integrating with all circumstances in all situations. In Dzogchen there is nothing to renounce; we must integrate with the negative as well as the positive. To be able to do this is to be a true Dzogchen practitioner. But we must realize that being free to do everything also means being free not to do things; otherwise, if we feel we have to do everything, this becomes another form of conditioning.

In order to attain complete realization, we must integrate with everything around us in the external world, but we must not stop at this point. It is very important to integrate with our passions. If we get angry, we must learn to integrate the anger, otherwise we simply start doing all the things we usually do when we are conditioned by anger. If this happens, the energy of the anger is of no use whatsoever to our practice. Likewise, we must integrate all the emotional states of joy and sadness, doubt and expectations, all the emotional obstacles, and everything in the waking state and the sleeping state. Finally, at the moment of death, we must integrate with death itself. This is the ultimate integration and is the attainment of realization.

Three Levels of Integration

A text from the *Zhang Zhung Nyan Gyud* called "The Mirror of the Luminous Mind" describes three ways of integrating everyday activities with presence. These correspond to the three levels of practitioners. In order to simplify understanding, these can usually be explained in this way.

At the highest level, as superior practitioners, we perform all our actions while constantly abiding in the state of non-dual presence. If we do not have this capacity, then, at the intermediate level, as average practitioners, we apply the wisdom of meditation to all our actions. If we are not able to do this, then, at the lowest level, as inferior practitioners, we make a commitment to carry out all the activities of our daily life with the mindful intention to benefit all sentient beings.

Corresponding to these are three levels of view (*lta ba*): the final or absolute view; the individual or meditation view; the mindfulness or conceptual awareness view.

The first is the highest view and concerns the highest practitioner. Here there is integration of all actions with the absolute state of nondual presence. This means we are able to effortlessly remain in the state of contemplation and to bring absolute wisdom and non-conceptual cognition into every action we perform. It is at this level that we can apply the Tibetan saying, "Non-meditation is the best meditation," because in meditation there is always effort involved to control and direct the mind. There is a story of a man who asked a Dzogchen master, "What do you practice?" The master answered, "There is nothing to practice." I also don't think there is anything to practice. Once you reach the state of knowledge, you are beyond practicing or not practicing. In terms of sense perception, here we not only experience the outer form of sense objects but we also perceive and experience their inner space, which is their inherent emptiness. In this case we directly integrate subject and object with the empty condition of the mind through our six sense consciousnesses and the inherent emptiness of phenomenal existence.

If we are not capable of directly integrating contemplation with our experience of every action we perform, then we must start at the second level, that of the average practitioner who meditates and applies the effort of insightful observation. We apply effort to remain in the state of contemplation and work by applying the view and wisdom of meditation to the subtle movements of energy during and immediately after our sessions of practice. A Tibetan proverb says: "Through meditation the practitioner observes and becomes naturally free." If we are not able to do this, then we must start at the third level, the lowest and humblest level, in which we work with the view of mindful attention and apply conceptual awareness to everything we do with our body, say with our voice, and think with our mind. In this case, as soon as we notice we are distracted, we apply greater effort of mindfulness to return to the state of contemplative awareness and, by conceptual reasoning, try to integrate the distracting thought or passion in the state of contemplation.

Practically speaking, the third level is actually the most useful one at which to start, in terms of communication with other people and direct awareness of others. What often happens if we try immediately to apply the highest level is that we live in a kind of fantasy of the absolute truth of emptiness and of the unreality of phenomena and thereby neglect to practice the relative truth of compassion towards others and we fail to develop awareness of our own and others' condition in the dualistic realm. In fact, this is the necessary and prior step to the highest integration. So it is best to start from the view of mindfulness and develop conceptual awareness in order gradually to discard it and finally achieve the capacity to integrate non-conceptual awareness with actions.

The three ways of integrating contemplation with actions correspond to practitioners of superior, average, and inferior ability.

The superior practitioner, whether master or disciple, has the greatest capacity to deal with the actions of body, voice, and mind from the absolute view in which there is neither samsara nor nirvana but complete emptiness. It is like acting in dreams where there is neither death nor the fear of death. This view is beyond all limits, so all actions are good. As nobody in the dualistic condition is free of limitations, it is important not to judge others' limitations but rather to try to see our own, and particularly to see them according to this final view. However, if we try to act according to this view before we are ready, we will become confused because we are still limited and yet attempting to act from the final view. This merely extends the dimension of our own limitations instead of being a way of definitively escaping from the fundamental limitation.

The average practitioner deals with the actions of body, speech, and mind by recognizing the six sense objects and liberates them by accepting them without conceptually grasping these sense perceptions. For example, the eye sense consciousness and conceptual cognition perceive the color white in different ways. Liberating the sense perception means not following after the perception with thought, thereby not grasping it with conceptual cognition. This corresponds to the individual meditation view in which we integrate actions by perceiving without grasping, not following perceptions with thought but instead liberating them. In fact, it is not perceptions but the mind that creates attachment and problems, by judging and making choices. In general, in simpler situations where there are fewer choices, there is less desire and attachment and therefore less confusion, fewer complications, and less conditioning.

Other systems, such as the Sutra system, do not consider the sense consciousnesses to be important, but in Dzogchen they are considered very important because the presence of mind manifests through all the sense consciousnesses, and it is through the sense consciousnesses that we can discover presence in our practice. In fact, it is easier to discover and realize self-presence through sense perception that is fresh and immediate than through thought that elaborates perception by conceptualization. When there is more presence with greater sensation, there is more feeling of integration. According to the Sutra system, the sense consciousnesses and their objects arise simultaneously from the movement of a karmic trace in the previous moment of mind. According to Dzogchen, the six sense consciousnesses are a manifestation of the Nirmanakaya. According to The *Zhang Zhung Nyan Gyud*, "From innate self-awareness wisdom that is light, through the movement of energy, the six sense consciousnesses and the six sense consciousness objects arise"; that is, they arise from presence (*rig pa*). When we remain in presence, the eye sense consciousness perceives light; the eye sense consciousness is not self-awareness but it perceives through presence.

The great eighth-century master Dranpa Namkhai advised: The five sense consciousnesses should not follow after the five objects; if they do follow after them, you should not make judgments with your mind. If your mind does make a judgment, do not grasp it as inherently existent; if you do grasp it, do not develop it into a gross passion.

He identified the steps we go through when we have a problem in practice and advised us to interrupt the steps, to retrace the steps back to where we first perceive an object and to leave it there as it is, without getting more and more involved with it. This advice is especially useful for the inferior practitioner whose practice and understanding are weak. In this case, when we perceive through the six sense consciousnesses, we should try to recognize the perceiver and the perceived. When we succeed in doing this, we see the object as in a mirror, we recognize the mirror and the object in the mirror. Seeing the mirror means seeing the object as the reflection of our self-presence. We must not get distracted even for an instant, even the time it takes to snap our fingers.

As inferior practitioners we work at the level of mindfulness through attention, by applying conceptual awareness to the acts we perform in everyday situations: to our relationships with our master, with other disciples, and with our family, and we try to keep them positive by maintaining awareness of how our actions have good or bad effects on others and on the surrounding situation, the earth, and the natural environment. Actually, this kind of constant mindful attention is much more powerful and effective than reciting mantras. Being aware of others is an antidote to negative actions, and working with our mind in this way brings about a positive change in ourselves.

The third column in the table is headed "state." At the absolute level, as superior practitioners, we practice in such a way that there is no mental effort and we remain continuously and undistractedly in the contemplative state of non-conceptual, non-dual presence through all activities. Everything we do takes place in total, innate awareness; nothing happens that is separate from that awareness, so everything is integrated; there is a continuity of awareness when we think, when we move, when we eat, and in all our activities. If we do not have this capacity, it means our practice is confined to limited periods of practice. As individual practitioners at the level of individual meditation, that is, as average practitioners, we apply the meditative insight that the mind is like a mirror that reflects perceptions. We do not grasp or judge perceptions. By not judging or grasping perceptions, we liberate them. At the level of mindful attention, as inferior practitioners, we apply conceptual awareness to actions so as not to follow them with thoughts. From the view of absolute contemplation, all actions are performed and self-liberated in the actionless state. From the perspective of individual meditation, actions are liberated by perceiving them without grasping; from the perspective of mindfulness, actions are liberated by addressing to them the attention of conceptual awareness.

Three Ways of Liberation

The next columns list the ways or styles of liberation and give examples. According to the level of the practitioner, there are three styles of liberating arising thoughts or passions. The superior practitioner has the greatest understanding of the fundamental base (*kun gzhi*), the source of samsara and nirvana, where both samsara and nirvana are self-perfected. We do not need to do anything to liberate thoughts because there is no judgment in this state. We are totally integrated in presence so there are no limitations to our activities. This style of liberation is primordial liberation or self-arising self-liberation. Here, thoughts and passions spontaneously self-liberate into the empty space of the mind simultaneously and effortlessly, immediately upon arising. This is the state of the complete realization of the Dzogchen masters, who walk, talk, eat, and do everything without being distracted or influenced by thought.

At the second level, that of the average practitioner, liberation is by self-observation when a sense perception or a passion such as anger arises. In this case there is effort involved because we do something to try to integrate: when we get angry, we try to remain in the state of contemplation or try to observe the passion and liberate it within ourselves. We liberate it when we see that the real nature of the passion is emptiness, just as the real nature of our mind is emptiness. The observer and the observed passion dissolve in the same moment, and we find ourselves in that union and try to remain in there with awareness. We try to see things as they are instead of being taken over by the passion. This style of liberation is called liberation upon arising. It requires the effort of observation and recognition of the passion, but not the use of an antidote (such as love or renunciation to overcome anger, as in the Sutric system, or visualization of a deity as in the Tantric system) in order to self-liberate.

At the third level, that of the inferior practitioner, there is the greatest difficulty in integrating with the state of contemplation and self-liberating thoughts and passions. We must try to work more with mindful awareness in connection with the body and the senses, recognizing passions when they arise and then not following after them. For example, when a passion arises, we can work with it by asking ourselves whether it has beneficial or harmful effects for ourselves and for others. Simply acknowledging that a passion such as anger has arisen is not enough, because it is easy to forget all our plans to work with anger once we have become angry. We have to recognize that passion is illusory like a dream; that is why the attention has to be mindful. This is liberation through bare, mindful attention and requires the effort of applying mindfulness in order not to follow the thoughts and passions.

We can take the sense perception of hearing a sound as an example. If the ear sense consciousness hears a sound, whether beautiful or unpleasant, there are three ways of dealing with it. The first, the superior practitioner's way is to allow the sound to self-liberate, freeing it by leaving it in the state of presence as it arises. This is natural self-liberation. The second, the average practitioner's way, is to liberate the sound by recognizing it on arising; this is "self-liberation on arising." The third, the inferior practitioner's way, is deliberately not to follow the sense perception with the mind when it has arisen. This is "self-liberation by mindful attention."

For the ordinary person, when a passion arises, there is no practice or presence. The passions can be brought into practice in three stages. At the first stage, when a passion arises, one remembers to practice and is able to remain aware while the passion is occurring. At the second stage, one spontaneously integrates with the passion and begins to be comfortable with its presence. Finally, at the third stage, the passion should actually awaken presence and help us to remain in presence, making the presence more stable and profound. We are human beings and should have the five passions, which are the expressions of the energy of our natural karmic condition. If we are able to understand their nature, then they become an ornament of our practice. This identity of presence and passion is the principle known as "one taste."

There are three examples of the three different ways of integration or liberation of the passions. In the case of the superior practitioner, the base of the mind (*kun gzhi*) is compared to an ocean, and a passion that arises from the empty space of the mind is compared to a snowflake falling into the ocean. The snowflake is of the same nature as the ocean, just as a passion is of the same empty nature as the mind. The ocean dissolves and integrates the snowflake automatically and without effort just as without effort the superior practitioner integrates and liberates all manifestations of the movements of the mind: thoughts and passions arise, abide, and self-liberate in the *kunzhi* base.

There is another example used for this effortless self-liberation: a knotted snake thrown in the air that effortlessly unties its knots as it falls to the ground. This example was attacked by a Gelugpa scholar who was a critic of Dzogchen. He said the example was unsuitable because the knotted snake thrown into the air is not the same snake that unties itself as it falls onto the earth. It is not the same snake in the sense that the snake does not exist permanently but changes from one moment to the next. However, in Dzogchen we do not say that the example of the snake suggests the existence of a permanent self, but that there is a continuity of moments of existence of the self. For example, if we order a ring from a goldsmith, we must pay him when he gives us the ring. But are we paying the wrong person? Is he the same goldsmith that made the ring? He is not the "same" goldsmith, but a continuation of that goldsmith. This is the same as the continuation of the snake: it is important to recognize this continuation of self in order to understand self-liberation.

In the case of the average practitioner, the arising of passion is compared to frost that needs heat to melt it. The heat is the observer in the mind that melts the passion, so some effort is needed for the observation and recognition of the passion as it arises and dissolves. There is effort involved. It is not sufficient just to say, "This is self-liberation" because that doesn't work: we have to do something.

In the case of the inferior practitioner, I have devised an example in addition to the one found in the original text: this is an illustration of how elements of the teachings can change with changing circumstances. In fun-fairs (and also in gambling casinos) in the United States there is a game that consists in hitting with a hammer targets that appear in the form of heads. If you're fast, there is enough time to hit all the heads as soon they come up. When I played this game, I found it a good analogy for the arising of thoughts. If we are not able to continue in the state of contemplation or to integrate the passions when they arise in everyday life, then we must try to notice them and somehow deal with them after they have arisen, so we "hit the passions." The more traditional example in the text says that we must come to an agreement between ourselves and our thoughts and passions. For example, if a passion like jealousy arises, we talk with the jealousy and ask, "Why are you so excited? There is no need to arise in this excited state and disturb me!" We try to observe and communicate with the passion and prove that it has no reason to come and disturb us. In this way we come to an agreement with it, with ourselves, and with useless or unnecessary thoughts that disturb our life and practice. If we are not capable of integrating in the superior or the average way, then we must succeed in coming to an agreement with our thoughts in order to have a good base as practitioners, and also as human beings.

As regards the three ways of self-liberation of the passions, if we are inferior practitioners, we must not think that every time a

passion like anger arises there is the self-liberation of anger because we have listened to many Dzogchen teachings about integration and the self-liberation of the passions and because we
consider ourselves Dzogchen practitioners. We have to find and
apply a precise practice suitable to our capacity and situation in
order to liberate and integrate the passions, otherwise we are
merely fooling ourselves. However, if self-liberation does not work
for us, this does not mean that it is not valid: it is valid for the
superior practitioner. It does not work for us because we have not
yet developed that capacity, because we make dualistic judgments
and are conditioned by circumstances too much.

Practical Advice on Integration

It is very important to discover through self-observation which
level of integration we are capable of practicing and to apply that
level, otherwise there will be a gap between the Dzogchen teachings and our aspirations as Dzogchen practitioners. When my
master Lopon Tenzin Namdak gave teachings on the *Zhang Zhung
Nyan Gyud* in Italy in 1989 he said, "The teaching is Dzogchen, we
are not Dzogchen." He was speaking about the gap between the
explanation of the state or base given in the teachings and the dualistic condition in which we live in our conceptual mind. We can
easily see if this gap exists when a passion such as anger arises.
When we receive teachings, we learn about integration and
self-liberation, but very often there is no functional relationship
between what we have learned from the teachings about passions
and what happens inside us when a passion such as anger arises.
That means the teaching is not working, and the anger we feel
does not correspond to the anger we speak about according to the
teachings. In practical terms, this is the gap my master was talking
about. The moment a passion arises, we forget all explanations. To
eliminate this gap, when we try to apply integration it is important not to follow blindly what the texts tell us about self-liberation,
but rather to first look at our own condition and determine at what
stage of practice we are, what level of practitioner we are, and then
apply the appropriate view and practice. It is as if we are sick. We
have to find out what illness we have and what kind of medicine
we must take. So the first step we must take towards integration is

to determine what level we have to work on, and not try immediately to apply the highest view of the teachings on integration and self-liberation, otherwise the gap will arise between the teaching and our capacity to apply it in the way we live. In this way, integration is one thing, and what we do is something else. We must connect what we learn about liberating the passions in the teachings and what we actually experience when we feel the passions arising.

If we find we are unable to integrate our passions, this is probably because we are confused about our level. Instead of applying the appropriate practice, we are trying to apply the superior practice while we are still on the inferior level. This might cause us to interrupt or even give up practice saying, "This teaching does not work," when in fact we are not applying it in the right way.

In fact, it is best to start with the lowest level of practice, of mindful attention to all our actions of body, voice, and mind. At times we can observe how we only notice the actions of our body after having performed them. For example, I may get up to walk out of the shrine room and accidentally kick somebody, then curse someone else for being in my way, and finally think badly of both people, before even stepping outside the door! I have performed these negative actions of body, voice, and mind with distraction, and this creates problems within myself. In fact, if I kick someone, I am kicking myself, as in the Tibetan saying, "If you hit a stone with butter, the butter loses; if you hit butter with a stone, the butter loses." In the end it is always I who loses. Often, we do negative things not because we have bad intentions, but because we are inattentive, but the effect is the same. So when we start to practice, we must first develop mindfulness, that is, effortful attention to the actions we perform, as a kind of base. Developing this lowest level of integration practice will help us to develop our capacity for the second level, where only the slight effort of bare observation and recognition are required for integration. When we have developed this quality, then remaining in contemplation becomes effortless, and integration becomes spontaneous. But if we have not mastered simple mindfulness, I am certain that continuity of awareness will be very difficult, because it means we are not applying the basic things. We are not applying mindfulness but are trying to understand continuity in the state of contemplation intellectually. Often we pass all our time as practitioners trying to remain in the state of contemplation without first trying to find out what we must do in order actually to succeed in doing so.

Attaining realization is not such a long path once we become able to integrate all our movements of energy in our practice, because then every action is governed by presence and becomes a step on the path and an expression of virtue. Practice is not only sitting in meditation, reciting mantras, or chanting. It is the application of practice in daily life that is most difficult, working with our energy in every life situation, with every sense perception, with every person we meet, whether we want to encounter that person or not.

9

Kunzhi
The Base of Everything

The *kunzhi* is like the sky
In the limitless dimensions.
Inherent wisdom shines like the sun in all directions.
The manifestations of the three *kayas*
Shine endlessly like sun-rays.

Kunzhi and Personal Experience

When we hear the primordial base explained in the context of
Dzogchen, it is good to match that explanation with our own personal experience of the base obtained through practice and the
master's introduction. Then the explanation will make sense and
will be something we can realize in ourselves. If we have not yet
had our own direct experience of the primordial base, rather than
forming conceptual ideas from explanations, it is better to do *zhiné*
practice and find the experience for ourselves.

In Dzogchen the *kunzhi* is the base of everything and corresponds to self-originated wisdom and to the enlightenment principle. This explanation is not the same as that of the *kunzhi* or *alayavijnana* in the Sutric Chittamatra system, where the *kunzhi* is described as a kind of mental consciousness that contains all the categories of thought and karmic traces that give rise to virtuous and nonvirtuous tendencies and actions.

In the *Zhang Zhung Nyan Gyud* the omnipervasiveness of the *kunzhi* is symbolized by space, limitless in extent and direction. Space is the infinite base of all existence. By *space* we mean the external space of the sky, the inner empty space of the mind, and the space inhabited by objects. Thus, according to the Bon teachings, this space is neither limited to external space nor to the space of the mind. In fact, in the *kunzhi* there is no distinction between inner and outer. When a form exists, such as a house, this form creates the difference between inner and outer, namely, the space inside and outside the house. The inner space seems to take form according to the shape of the house so that we talk about space that is square, triangular, oval, or round. The *kunzhi* totally and uniformly pervades both samsara and nirvana and is not divided into internal and external. It is the ordinary dualistic mind that distinguishes between inner *kunzhi*, the selflessness of the individual that is the empty nature of the mind, and the outer *kunzhi* that is the absolute reality of all existence. In reality these limits do not pertain. Just as the self-originated wisdom of the *kunzhi* pervades the mind of sentient beings, so it pervades all phenomenal existence and the whole universe. It expands and spreads in all directions without distinction of internal or external, center or boundary.

One simile in the *Zhang Zhung Nyan Gyud* likens the *kunzhi* of the mind to the sky, in which the sun, which represents innate awareness, shines clear and free of thoughts, which are likened to clouds. In essence there is no difference between the sky and the sun as there is no separation between the sunlight and the sky. It is because *rigpa* manifests in the empty space in the mind that we are able to realize the nature of the *kunzhi*.

But if the *kunzhi* is omnipervasive, inside and outside the mind, why does presence not manifest in external material phenomena as it does in the mind? We could say that it is because awareness is not present in external material phenomena. The sun shines in the sky but is only reflected in objects such as crystals and not in objects such as stones, which do not have the potentiality to reflect light. Likewise awareness can only manifest in the minds of sentient beings who have the potentiality to reflect it; external material phenomena do not have this potentiality.

If one thinks there is a contradiction between the *kunzhi*'s being "the single sphere of totality" and its pervading all things, this can be refuted with the example of the sun, which is reflected in all the seas and rivers. That there are many reflections does not mean there are many suns.

If one thinks there is a contradiction between the *kunzhi*'s being primordially pure and its being the repository of karmic traces and the source of ignorance, this can be refuted by understanding that the base is without the dualism of purity and impurity, which arises in the moving mind that draws distinctions. For example, space can be polluted but the pollution is in the mind of the observer only. Space itself remains space and does not change by being polluted. In the same way, pervading awareness remains pure; ignorance and the obscurations arise in consciousness awareness, which draws the distinction between understanding and ignorance. In the *kunzhi* both samsara and nirvana are spontaneously perfected.

One might think of the samsaric creativity of the individual as functioning like a corporation: our *kunzhi* base consciousness is our emotional bank account where we store our experiences and karmic traces and create our personality. It is like the corporate record books in that as a receptacle it is empty in itself but it receives the proceeds of the corporation's transactions. Our mind consciousness, motivated by samsaric desires, determines our purposes and aims. It is like the president of the corporation who determines the corporate goals and delegates responsibilities motivated by the need for power and profit. Our obscuration consciousness is the mind that grasps and holds its experiences and does not let them self-liberate. It is like the treasurer or efficiency-expert who jealously guards the company funds. Our five senses, directed by the desires and aims of our mind consciousness, conduct our relations with the world. They are like the staff and employees who mediate between the president and the marketplace.

In another simile from the *Zhang Zhung Nyan Gyud*, the *kunzhi* is likened to space, *rigpa* to a bird, the moving mind to wings, and the body to a net. Like a bird caught in a net, mind and body are joined together by karmic causes, but when the net breaks, the bird and the net separate and the bird flies away. In the same way when a person dies, the body and the mind separate. However, although net and bird separate, they are never separate from space: their coming together and separation take place in space. In the same way the mind and body are never separated from the *kunzhi* base. Here space represents the omnipresence of the primordial base and of the primordial awareness, always present in the mind regardless of whether the consciousness awareness is present or distracted.

10

Ma
The Mother

In conceptualizing faults and features of samsara and
  nirvana,
Ignorant erroneous conceptions differ from primordial wisdom.
Within the essential basis, these are not two.

Ma, Bu, and Tsal

In the *Zhang Zhung Nyan Gyud*, there is a twofold exposition of the
base of the primordial state: first, a brief discussion of the essential
teachings, and, second, a discussion of the generation of luminosity. The explanation of the essential teachings is given in three sections: the essence of the teaching, liberation through activity, and
liberation from illusion.

  The first of these three sections explains the base of the primordial state by discussing three topics: the mother (*ma*), the son (*bu*),

and energy (*tsal*), energy being the inseparability of the mother and son. Symbols such as "the mother and son" are used in Dzogchen to clarify and facilitate understanding. This triad corresponds to the triad widely used in the Nyingmapa Dzogchen teachings: essence (*ngo bo*), nature (*rang bzhin*) and energy (*thugs rje*). To some extent *ma* corresponds to the absolute truth, *bu* to the relative truth, and tsal to the unification of the two truths in the Sutra teachings found in the Prajnaparamita literature.

Ma is the *kunzhi*, the base (*gzhi*) of everything (*kun*). As the *kunzhi*, "*ma*" is a symbol for the emptiness of the natural state, experienced by the individual as the unborn essence of the mind; "*bu*" is the clarity (*rig pa*) of the natural state, experienced by the individual as unobscured wisdom, the luminous self-awareness of the mind. The empty space of the *kunzhi* is dark, and the clarifying light of *rigpa* arises and irradiates the *kunzhi*. The space remains empty but luminous — it is no longer dark. This arising luminous *rigpa* in the emptiness of the primordial state is the son of the mother-*kunzhi*-space. Thus *kunzhi* and *rigpa* are said to be like the inseparable mother and son. In the primordial state, emptiness and clarity are inseparable. In the primordial state, emptiness is unobscured. Emptiness is clarity and clarity is emptiness. We cannot say that emptiness is one thing and clarity another because, in fact, they are a single unity.

The Qualities and Aspects of Space

The analogy of the mother is used because all the phenomena of existence are born from the nature of the *kunzhi* and have their function and liberation in that nature. The mother is the fundamental base of all samsara and nirvana; at the absolute level, it is known as "bodhichitta" and as "the space of the nature of phenomena," because it has the nine qualities of space:

1. boundlessness
2. omnipervasiveness
3. unlimited expansiveness
4. being without top or bottom
5. immeasurableness
6. uncontractedness

7. great vastness
8. everlastingness
9. immutability

These nine qualities of space can also be explained as aspects of the three kinds of absolute emptiness or space, *kha* (*mkha'*), *long* (*klong*), and *ying* (*dbying*). *Kha* (*mkha'*) is external space conceived without consideration of the things contained within it; *long* (*klong*), is the space of the objects that exist within the *kha*; and *ying* (*dbying*) is the space of direct experience as such. These three can be translated as external space (*mkha'*), internal space (*klong*), and secret space (*dbying*). The three spaces are associated with three other terms: *kha* is associated with "example" space *be* (*dpe*), *long* with "significance" space (*don*), and *ying* with "sign" space (*rtags*).

Kha, or *be*-space, is external, empty space, open like the sky. (The word *kha* also means sky). *Long*, or *don*-space, is the space of objects in that they, too, are considered to be empty like the sky. To help us understand the empty nature of objects, we are given the "example" of external empty space, which we are to apply to objects. By applying this example of empty space to the object, we understand the significance of the assertion that objects, like external space, are empty. This mental understanding itself is a "sign" or indication (*rtags*) of "secret space": the space of mind that is also the integration of the three spaces, secretly found without trying to find it.

Kha, example space, is surrounding space, the external mother of the external son, and is the base of the internal space of existent, substantial phenomena. For example, empty space (*mkha'*) is the original basis for the manifestation of a cloud. *Kha*-space makes possible the movement of the elements, which, in turn, are the conditions of possibility for the manifestation of the cloud. The continuous development of the elements in inner space (*klong*) gives rise to the actual manifestation of the cloud. Even the elements that produce the cloud all arise in the dimension or state of empty space, without there ever being any separation between the movement giving rise to the development of the cloud and the space of the cloud, from which the movement manifests. All the movements — arising, development, function, liberation — of the cloud, the "external son," are based in external or surrounding space, which is the "external mother."

Meaning space — *long* or *don* — is inner space and is the natural condition of phenomena. All phenomena, particularly at the substantial level of existing things, originate from this internal space where the elements that bring about the production of phenomena manifest.

Sign space is connected with the secret or mental space, also known as Buddhahood. All moving thoughts originate from inner mental space: their arising, development, function, and liberation all take place inseparably from this space, which is the sunyata (emptiness) of the mind.

The absolute reality of every object, and of the mind itself, is emptiness: this is called "primordial purity" in Dzogchen and "absolute truth" in the Sutras. In the example of the sun and the crystal, the emptiness base of all reality, the absolute truth of existence, is like the sun that shines everywhere, while the emptiness base or space of the mind (*dbyings*) is like the crystal that is able to reflect the light of the sun. Only in the mind can emptiness understand itself.

Sky Gazing Practice

It is of great importance to have experiential, and not merely conceptual, understanding of the inseparability of external surrounding space, the internal space within objects, and the secret space in the mind. When the Dzogchen teachings talk about integrating the mind with space through the practice of gazing into the sky, the practitioner is trying to be present in the inseparability of these three spaces. The reason the practice is performed by gazing is not to limit sense perception to the visual sense consciousness only. It is possible to experience the inseparability of the three spaces through all the senses. The eye sense organ is favored because it is the most important of the five sense consciousnesses and because it is associated with the space element. It is through the eyes that we see the base wisdom while gazing into space. Inner luminosity originates in the heart and passes through two channels that connect the empty space of the heart with the external empty space of the sky through the eyes, the "water light doors" of the inner light. Thus it is through the eyes that the inner luminosity is projected into external space. In this way the space element of the heart, the space element of the eye sense consciousness, and the external surrounding space element of the sky are connected. This is integration with space, and we no longer feel limited by our bodies to one specific location but are present everywhere in space with no boundaries.

There are two traditional Tibetan examples used to show that outer space is a projection of inner space. The first is a house. If we shine a light inside a house, the light is projected out through the windows, just as the inner light is projected from the empty space of our internal elements through our sense consciousnesses into external space. The second is the placing of a butter lamp inside a puppet complete with holes for eyes and situated in a dark room. The light we can see shining through the apertures is the inner clear light of inner space, the light of presence we project through our eyes and through all the senses.

This is the union of mother and son.

The Four Qualities of the Mother

Ma, the *kunzhi*, has four qualities:

1. It possesses primordial purity.
2. It manifests spontaneous perfection.
3. It manifests neutrality.
4. It is the single sphere of totality.

The mother is said to have the quality of primordial purity because she is not tainted by any obscurations or by the dualisms of samsara and nirvana, virtue and nonvirtue, passions and blessings, conceptual thoughts and non-conceptual wisdom, happiness and suffering, inner and outer, subject and object, cause and effect, or by any bias towards good or bad.

She is said to have the quality of spontaneous perfection because, in her, all of samsara and nirvana, virtue and nonvirtue, passions and blessings, thought and wisdom, happiness and suffering, inner and outer, subject and object, cause and effect, and good and bad are primordially perfected.

She is said to be neutral because she is not biased towards virtue or nonvirtue, not limited in the arising of virtue or nonvirtue, and because she is the basis of the potentiality for the arising of everything.

She is said to be "the single sphere of totality" because she embraces all the three spaces: external space, internal space, and secret space, and, thus, also the spaces of example, meaning, and sign. Great external clear space is the unlimited mother without bias in regard to direction or time; internal space is the mother from which all substantial existence is born and by which all existents are produced; secret space is the mother-awareness of the non-duality of emptiness and clarity, the space of the condition of existence. She is called "single sphere of totality" because emptiness and clarity appear together in their subject, consciousness awareness, which itself is not separate from appearance.

In using a twofold classification of external and internal, we can say that when the great sphere of totality manifests externally it is called external space or "example." When it manifests internally, it is called secret space, the nature of the mind, and Buddhahood or "sign." When it manifests in the unity of external and internal, it is called internal space, the natural condition of phenomena or "meaning."

The Mother of All Existence

The *kunzhi* is the mother of all existence, the origin of nirvana and samsara, of inner and outer existence, of negative and positive, of enlightenment and illusion.

Although the base of all, the mother has no attributes, is without form or color, and is herself baseless. She is unborn, like the sky, not created by any activity, and without any cause. There is no substantial base giving rise to the primordial *kunzhi*; it is the inherent empty nature of everything. It is the space from which the elements, which are the fundamental structure of inner and outer existence, arise. It is the base of origination of all thoughts in the mind and all objects in external existence. It is the source of the three great visions, the sound, light, and rays, which are the manifestations of the energy of the natural state.

When it is said that the mother is the source of inner existence, this refers to the *kunzhi* as the nature of the mind, unborn and empty like the sky.

The Experience of the Mother in Meditation

We can have a direct experience of the inseparability of mother and son in our own practice. If we observe the origin of thoughts during meditation, we can see that they arise and dissolve in the natural base of the mind. If we are aware that they come from emptiness and leave them be, thoughts go away and we abide in the state of contemplation in which the emptiness that remains becomes clearer. That emptiness is the *kunzhi* and the clarity is *rigpa*, the clear awareness of emptiness in the state of contemplation. Their inseparability is the unity of emptiness and clear awareness in the natural state, just as the rays of sunlight are the energy that is the manifestation of the inseparability of the sun and the sky. Emptiness without clarity would be like sleeping. When we sleep, we are not present, but in practice we must maintain presence in the state. This has to be clarified in our practice. We must not try to have *rigpa* present in the *kunzhi*; we must be present in the inseparable state of *kunzhi* and *rigpa* in our contemplation. In the state of contemplation, we can realize the inseparability of *kunzhi* and *rigpa*, of emptiness and clarity, in which mother and son are happy to be reunited. In this reunion we feel a particular kind of joy. Now we have completed the stage of limited practice sessions and reach the stage where there is no separation between practice and non-practice. It is in reference to this stage that the Dzogchen teachings say that the best meditation is nonmeditation, meditation not fabricated by the mind's purposefulness. The final realization of wisdom, when *rigpa* is recognized as the manifestation of the energy of the *kunzhi*, is like the son returning to his mother's lap.

11

Bu
The Son

This primordially existing essence
Unrealized because we are unaware,
Is clearly seen once instruction is given,
As one whose face is unseen
Sees it when given a mirror.

The Qualities of the Son

Bu, the son, is known by the names of its different qualities: innate awareness (*rig pa*), nature (*ngo bo*), innately aware wisdom (*rang rig ye shes*), the base of everything of the moving mind (*shes rig rgyud kyi kun gzhi*).

The son is the unobscured self-awareness of the primordial state, a non-conceptual self-understanding wisdom that is beyond thought. If we say that the understanding of the state is beyond thought, who then understands the state? It is the state that understands itself. For example, a butter lamp (or in the West we could use the example of an electric light bulb) illuminates not only what is around it; it also illuminates itself. In the same way the state understands itself by its own intrinsic awareness. There is self-understanding because the natural state is not emptiness or awareness but the inseparability of emptiness and awareness, of mother and son, *ma* and *bu*, so the awareness understands the emptiness. Or, more properly, as they are inseparable, emptiness is awareness and awareness is emptiness, and emptiness understands itself by its own awareness. This emptiness cannot be understood by conceptual thought; thought can only understand the mental image of emptiness. This is the way used in the Sutra system initially to understand the empty nature of absolute reality. In Dzogchen it must be directly perceived and immediately understood by *rigpa*.

The son is the unobscured, self-clear essence of the empty nature of the non-grasping mind. It is the base of the manifestations of the moving mind. Its continuity is uninterrupted. If we know this mind, this mirror of awareness, all nirvanic qualities reflect or manifest in it. Because it has this quality, it is called the "mirror-like wisdom." If we do not have this knowledge, the mind becomes the source of samsara and the base where the karmic traces are stored.

Mother and Son Awareness

In the *Zhang Zhung Nyan Gyud* a distinction is drawn between self-arising wisdom and innately aware wisdom. The former is the mother, the self-arising wisdom of the base awareness. The latter is the son, self-arising wisdom of the energy awareness. It is important here to discuss self-awareness further. If we say that the mother and the son are never separated, this means *rigpa* is never distracted from awareness. How then does samsara arise? The nature of the mind is like the sea, and samsaric mind is like the moving waves of the sea. It is on the level of the moving mind that samsara exists. It is the moving mind that distinguishes reality into samsara and nirvana.

Three Kinds of Rigpa

There are three different kinds of awareness (*rig pa*): pervading awareness (*chab rig*); consciousness or moving-mind awareness (*bsam rig*); and primordial awareness (*ye rig*). Pervading awareness (*chab rig*) is inseparable from the *kunzhi* base and is omnipresent in all material existence. Moving-mind awareness is the son *rigpa* found only in the mind of sentient beings, in whom distraction can interrupt the continuity of awareness. When we are distracted, we cannot remain in the state of contemplation. Primordial awareness is the mother *rigpa*, the awareness that is always present whether we practice or not. This is the awareness that the moving-mind awareness is trying to comprehend. We should not think, however, that since pervading awareness is omnipresent and since primordial awareness is ever-present, there is no need to practice. It is the innate but unknown individual awareness that we need to encounter and develop and that the master introduces once we discover it in ourselves.

It is possible for moving-mind awareness to understand primordial awareness because of the inseparability of mother and son and because the ever-present, self-existing, primordial awareness is not something the moving-mind awareness creates but simply discovers.

Sky Gazing Practice

Primordial awareness is projected and reflected through the five senses. It is experienced through the five sense consciousnesses and, in particular, through the eye sense consciousness because of the relationship between the elements associated with inner organs, sense organs, and sense consciousnesses. In the case of the eyes, the relationship is with the space element and with the heart.

element	space
inner organ	heart
sense consciousness	sight
sense organ	eye
object of sense perception	form

This association of elements with the senses is one of the underlying principles of the practice of sky gazing. Primordial awareness knows no development or decline, but there is a time when the practice of gazing into space goes well and a time when it does not. Obstacles may arise, such as drowsiness or agitation, lack of clarity or lack of the experience of emptiness. In order to overcome these kinds of obstacles, it is recommended to change the kind and direction of the gaze. To overcome drowsiness, we should apply the wrathful gaze, looking upwards; to overcome the problem of agitation, we should apply the peaceful gaze, looking downwards. To develop method, we should gaze to the left; to develop wisdom, to the right.

It can be said that when we experience the fruition of the sky gazing practice we are seeing primordial awareness itself through our physical eyes, experiencing and realizing it while the moving-mind awareness is continuously and undistractedly present through the eye sense consciousness. In this way we develop the *trekchö* contemplation practice of remaining in union with space (discussed in Chapter 15). When we have realized stability in *trekchö*, we should engage in unification with space whereby the potential quality of the element lights can manifest, using particular methods such as the "forced introduction of the clear light," or by gazing into the space where sky and mountain meet, or directly into the blue sky, or at the moon, the sun, or by doing the *tögel* dark retreat. In this case we no longer remain only in integration with space but experience the movement of energy within the experience of space. This is the principle of *tögel* practice. When we develop *tögel* practice, the eye sense organ is the main sense "door" through which we experience the movement of energy in space. In the Sutra system we cannot find descriptions of this kind: this explanation and these practices are unique to Dzogchen. However, it is important as aspirant practitioners to remember that we should get precise pointing out instructions from a competent Dzogchen master before starting to do these practices.

In the *Zhang Zhung Nyan Gyud* system, six examples are given by the master during the symbolic transmission to enable the practitioner to have direct, and not merely conceptual, understanding of the different qualities of *bu*, primordial awareness. These are not mere philosophical discriminations of its qualities. The natural state is a single totality, and we should spontaneously and directly experience every aspect without the conceptual mind drawing distinctions: this is the way of direct transmission through symbols. Sometimes symbols can be much more effective than clarification through intellectual descriptions because, although we learn through intellectual descriptions, we grow through symbols; they are not "forced" like conceptual explanations. This is especially true of the *Zhang Zhung Nyan Gyud*, where most of the elucidations are given through symbols rather than intellectual explanations.

These six qualities of the son are:

1. The butter lamp, which is the symbol of self-clarity;
2. The lotus, which is the symbol of primordial purity;
3. The peacock feather, which is the symbol of the spontaneous perfection of the clear light;
4. The mirror, which is the symbol of the unobscured self-clarity;
5. The crystal, which is the symbol of the naked transparent wisdom (lit. "transparent nakedness");
6. Space, which is the symbol of impartial, omnipervasive wisdom.

There is self-understanding, self-presence, self-clarity. Often when the teachings use the terms "clarity" or "clear light" we tend to think of a pure light, but it is not like that. Clarity means knowing ourselves, rather than knowing some object or thing or knowing ourselves as an object. Here the self, the soul, and the person are the same, and the inherent space of all three is emptiness. It is because emptiness is the inherent nature of the self that we say "absence of self." There is no permanent or independent self in the self or in phenomena. The traditional example is of a farmer that looks for a yak and cannot find it: what he finds is "no yak." When we search for a "self" and do not find one, what we find is "no self"; this means finding our true self.

Even though the lotus grows in the mud, its purity is never sullied by the mud; likewise the lotus-like purity of primordial awareness is never contaminated by the mud-like passions. The primordial purity of the mind is the primordial Buddha,

Kuntuzangpo, pure even though involved with the poisons of thoughts and passions. Just as waves are of the same quality as the sea, so the passions are of the same quality as purity and wisdom. Once we understand that purity is their true quality, then we see that they are never separate from purity.

It is not an artist that paints the colors and lights on peacock feathers; in the same way the lights and elements, that are the origin of existence and of samsara and nirvana, are not created by anyone but are spontaneously perfected. The primordial state is spontaneously perfected beyond concepts and beyond time. These latter are products of the conceptual mind; this means it is perfect all the time, and right now. It is the conceptual mind that separates samsara and nirvana and classifies things as "good" (nirvanic) and "bad" (samsaric). But it is because both samsara and nirvana are self-perfected in the primordial state that they can manifest at all.

As a mirror is not obscured by any bias or judgment when it reflects what appears before it, primordial awareness is not obscured by the appearance of objects or conceptual thoughts.

A crystal is naked and translucent; in the same way primordial awareness is bare of any conceptual thoughts, and internal and external experiences are transparent to the observing primordial awareness.

Space is beyond "inner" and "outer"; it is omnipervasive and beyond direction, just as primordial awareness can be found in every sentient being.

Although symbols and other types of non-conceptual clarifications do not capture the final understanding, they are more immediate and easier to understand than philosophical explanations. When the master introduces the natural state of mind to the disciple through these six symbols, this should enable the disciple to experience each individual quality of the son during the master's transmission.

12

Tsal
Energy

Once hatred is renounced, love cannot be discerned —
The single nature of the mind renounces nothing.
Once ignorance is renounced, wisdom cannot be
    discerned —
The single nature of the mind renounces nothing.
Once desire is renounced, generosity cannot be
    discerned —
The single nature of the mind renounces nothing.

The Three Great Visions

The Dzogchen teachings explain that the movement of energy (*tsal*)
in the primordial state gives rise to light in the form of the five
pure lights, and when it increases, "the sound of light" arises. The
five lights are the base of the manifestations of the clear light energy in the form of sound, light, and rays, called the "three great

visions" or "three great movements." These are the expressions of the energy of *rigpa*.

The Self-appearance of the Three Great Visions

The *Zhang Zhung Nyan Gyud* describes the self-appearance of these three great visions. The appearance of the inherent self-sound of awareness is like an echo: like a sound that seems to come from somewhere else but, in fact, is returning to its source.

The appearance of the inherent self-light of awareness is like a rainbow that arises, remains, and dissolves in the sky. Observing a rainbow (or a cloud) when it appears in the sky, we can understand how the movement of energy in the mind, whether in the form of a thought or a passion, occurs in the same way: it arises from the empty state, which is the inherent nature or essence of the mind (and also the inherent nature of thoughts and of the passions), dwells in the empty nature of the mind, and finally dissolves back into the empty nature of the mind.

The appearance of the inherent self-rays of awareness is compared to images seen in a mirror, or a statue that we recognize as soon as we see it; it is like the magical apparition of a body. The rays are rays of light, analogous to the rays of sunlight that come from the sun, without this implying that "first" there is the sun and "then" the appearance of the rays coming from it: the sun and the rays of sunlight are simultaneous.

We truly understand the sound, light, and rays to be the manifestations of the energy of our own primordial state, and the expression of our awareness when we perceive them in the state of presence, in the state of *rigpa*, self-awareness. When the three great visions arise, we understand them as the external arising of our own awareness as if we were looking in a mirror. When we look in a mirror, we see our face and recognize ourselves; likewise, when we truly see the nature of the three great visions, we perceive them as the projected manifestations of the natural state, as projections of the light of the mind. According to the *Zhang Zhung Nyan Gyud*, the light of the mind is like the open sky seen over a hill. If we sit on a hilltop and gaze out to where the sky meets another hill, and if we see how they join, move, and change, and how the mountain changes into colors, becoming more and more the reflection of our mind, we are seeing our own mind moving. This becomes very clear also if we gaze into the sky: we see its interpenetrating aspects, and the states of purity and impurity are clearly delineated.

These visions are the cause of our understanding our own condition. In Dzogchen this is self-understanding: we understand not only ourselves but also all phenomena as our own manifestation. The difference between nirvana and samsara is the difference between understanding and not understanding, so that if we understand the nature of the three great visions when they arise in the after-death *bardo*, the process of realization starts; whereas, if we don't understand, we return to samsara.

Experiencing the Sound, Light, and Rays in Practice

We can have direct experience and knowledge of the self-arising of the three great visions in our own practice. For example, if we block our ears with our fingers, we hear the natural self-sound. In this way we experience the connection between sound and emptiness because the clear light of emptiness is the base where the three great visions arise. There are particular techniques to produce the experience of light such as by looking at the sun, gazing into the sky, or doing the dark retreat. An easier way is to close our eyes and press our eyeballs slightly with our fingers so that we see the natural, self-arising light. This is the inner light. There is an infinite number of different visions we can see in this way, such as five-colored circles of light, light beads (*thigle*), images, stupas, or mandalas. Whatever is present in the mind can manifest as vision. When we project the light outwards, it manifests as the visible forms (people, houses etc.) that we see. They are produced by the gross elements but their true quality is the pure light of the primordial condition. Likewise, inner sound manifests externally as music, noise, and so forth. If we practice blocking our ears, pressing our eyeballs, and holding our breath while remaining in the state of presence, we can then release the pressures and see the inner light and hear the inner sound. Everything manifests in that moment. When we release the breath, it is calm and relaxing and we remain in the state of self-presence.

It is important to understand the difference between hearing external sounds and doing this exercise. When we block our ears, we must try to be present in the inner sound and see in what way it is different, for instance, from hearing a film sound-track. Another practice related to sound requires us to block our ears for a week, until a loud inner sound starts to arise. Then we can integrate with the sound of an element or combine the practice with light by pressing the eyes, in order to enter into a state of self-presence. This is called the "secret place of sound" or the "sound of *rigpa*." This practice is especially useful during a dark retreat, in which visions usually arise first. We can then integrate with sounds when they start to speak. When doing these practices, we begin by holding our breath, but we do not have to go on holding the breath to have total presence: we release the breath and remain present. In this way we can see that total, continuous presence will not interfere with our everyday life. We should not think that integration means remaining in the state of attention while holding the breath: through our experience of the presence that remains after releasing the breath, we understand presence in purposeful tension and the difference between presence and this tension, so that we can apply presence outside the situation of the deliberate intentions we have during a practice session.

Four Analogies from the *Zhang Zhung Nyan Gyud*

The *Zhang Zhung Nyan Gyud* uses four analogies as examples of the self-arising manifestations of energy. These are water, a crystal, the sun, and a butter lamp.

In the first example, the sun shines on water so that its image is reflected onto a wall. Concentrating on the final, external image, we lose contact with the connection between the sun, the source of the image, and the image of the sun on the wall. The water is like emptiness, the light on the water bearing the image of the sun is like *rigpa* self-awareness, and the light reflected from the water is like the manifestation of the energy that appears as external. In this example it is important to understand that the light reflected on the water is empty and clear and its nature is not different from the water, just as waves in the sea are of the same nature as the sea itself. In the same way, the three visions are the light of *rigpa* projected externally: they are the reflections of *rigpa*. In this example, the sun also represents the primordial state, present in all existence but only perceptible as *rigpa* self-awareness in the mind, just as the light of the sun shines everywhere but is only reflected by certain objects or surfaces, such as, in this example, water. In fact, the sun reflected on the wall does not exist. It is just a reflection of the mind.

The second example is a crystal. We do not have to do anything artificial to produce light in a crystal: the crystal is spontaneously self-perfected, and, when the sun shines, light will naturally manifest from the crystal, just as the three great visions, the display of the energy of the primordial state, manifest as projections of *rigpa*. In this example, the sun is a secondary cause: without it there is no manifestation. For instance, if I see a "good" or "bad" person, the goodness or badness is not inherent but actuated by the secondary cause: in himself the person is self-perfected, just as the crystal is. A person can be, at the same time, father, son, husband, friend, and enemy to a number of different people; his inherent condition is the same, but he will manifest differently according to the secondary circumstances of those other persons" perceptions of him.

The third example is the sun. The sun symbolizes the innate self-awareness. The sun, shining in the sky, symbolizes the empty nature of the mind. In this case the three great visions are the sunlight. In daily life we see forms, hear sounds, and generally perceive external reality and objects through our senses. If we perceive these with awareness, present in the inseparability of emptiness and clarity, we see them as our own manifestation, as the self-manifestation of the energy of our primordial state. If thought distracts us from presence, we see them as separate from ourselves, as originating externally and not as our own externalized projections.

In terms of practice in general, but particularly when we do a *tögel* dark retreat, we should try to perceive the manifestations of sound, light, and rays as productions of our own energy and not as something outside of ourselves. In this way it is possible to recognize outer reality as ultimately our own projection, thereby uniting "inner" vision and "outer" objective reality. This helps us to develop inner wisdom. There are many stories of practitioners who do dark retreats and mistake their mind-produced visions for external reality. What is important is not the content or form of the visions that appear, whether what arises in the vision is a Buddha or an animal, but how we observe it, and whether we can recognize what we experience as the manifestation of the energy of our own primordial state. It is also important for us to obtain this realization in the dark retreat in order to learn how to recognize the visions of the peaceful and wrathful deities that arise as our own projections in the *bardo*. When we achieve this, it is the awakening of understanding. If we recognize the vision of the five pure lights, the process of nirvana begins. If we do not understand the nature of the lights, these coarsen, give rise to the five material elements, and start the process of samsara.

The fourth example is the butter lamp that illuminates itself as well as what lies around it. It represents self-clarity, the self-understanding of emptiness that comprehends visions as the manifestation of its own clarity. This is the natural state understanding itself by its own inherent clarity. This "self-understanding wisdom" is the expression of the inseparability of mother and son in the primordial state.

Experiencing the Three Great Visions

When the three great visions arise, it is important not to follow after them. It is crucial to distinguish between following after them and accepting but not following after them. Following after them means being conditioned by whether they are positive or negative, beautiful or ugly. Accepting them means allowing them to arise and watching them with presence, observing them without attachment or aversion.

If we do not follow after them, then the great visions are under control and no problems can arise. We see them, we appreciate and even enjoy the visions, but we are not influenced by them because we remain present. If our mind is not distracted by the three visions when they arise in the *bardo*, then the process of nirvana begins. It is important to experience directly that visions are our own manifestation.

When our mind directly understands the three great visions, they become the cause for our individual presence and we realize we are king of our own state. Nothing is capable of distracting us from our true condition.

Relating with Energy

The *Zhang Zhung Nyan Gyud* also explains how to deal with energy in relation to secondary causes, the activities of everyday life, so that we learn how to use the events of our daily life as part of our practice. It also explains how to apply the practices learned during our lifetime to the manifestations of the energy of secondary causes that arise in the *bardo*.

Relating with energy during our lifetime means working with the three principal dimensions of body, speech, and mind, working with the six sense consciousnesses, working with thoughts, and working with all the problems and limitations within ourselves.

Relating with energy in terms of integration has three possible approaches that correspond to the three types or levels of practitioners: superior, average, and inferior. There are two ways of dealing with energy: the first is appropriate in the early stages of practice and the second in the later stages. When we start to practice, we are in the condition of the inferior practitioner. We are like a butter lamp that can be blown out by the wind; that is, our practice can easily be distracted by movements of energy such as thoughts or passions. For this reason, all our activities of body, voice, and mind should be positive and virtuous and we should renounce any experience that is an obstacle to practice rather than immediately trying to integrate it. We are advised to seek only those things and circumstances (work, home, thoughts, food, drink) that will prove beneficial to practice and avoid those that could prove hindrances. It is at this stage that we do the *ngondro, powa,* guru yoga, and other preliminary and purificatory practices. However, once we have established and developed our practice, instead of being like a butter lamp, we become like a big fire, so that the big wind of the movement of energy is no longer an obstacle to practice but rather helps the fire (our practice) to burn stronger and brighter.

"Zerbu"

There is a text in the *Zhang Zhung Nyan Gyud* specifically on the subject of energy and actions called *Zerbu*. *Zerbu* means, literally, "hitting a nail" to fasten something, and, symbolically, to "fix" the actions of body, speech, and mind in everyday life to our level of practice. I will paraphrase and comment upon key passages from this text.

When a vision is an obstacle, you need a friend.

"Vision" refers to the movements of energy; the friends we need are renunciation and the preliminary practices. But when vision is no longer a hindrance, we reach a different stage. Once we have developed our practice, former obstacles become of benefit to our practice.

When a fire grows and becomes a big blaze, then wind helps the fire.

At this stage we actually need the wind, the movements of energy, so that instead of stagnating, we can develop our practice, and for this we need the energy of thoughts and passions to integrate with contemplation. The use of the passions through complete integration with them is called "crazy wisdom."

Self-arising wisdom is the base.

All movements of energy, whether subtle thoughts or gross passions, arise in the base and take place in the state of presence. We must maintain undistracted presence of awareness, identifying the six sense consciousnesses as self-arising wisdom each time we try to integrate with a movement of body, voice, or mind.

The five poisons are energy.

All movements of thought, all the passions, are energy in powerful, visible form.

Following after the five poisons is illusion.

To follow after passions would mean not recognizing their inherent reality, which is emptiness.

Seeing the five poisons as negative is a mistake.

This means not recognizing them as the manifestations of the energy of the primordial state.

Leaving passions in their own nature is the method.

This is the superior way of integrating passions when they arise; it is like a snowflake dissolving in the ocean.

Doing this, and obtaining the result which is understanding, is the path.

When you realize there is no separation between the passions and the pure state of the mind, that is the state of enlightenment.

This is the skillful Dzogchen method of using the passions without Tantrically transmuting them. By integrating these manifestations of energy, we understand their nature as the movements of our primordial state, and in this way they become the path of realization and liberation.

It is at this stage that we become free. Nothing disturbs us and we act according to "crazy wisdom." As the text says, we "behave like a pig or a dog" who has no dualistic considerations. Good, bad, clean, dirty, everything is perceived as having "one taste." Another text says that at this stage we become "like a little child who does not know anything and will do anything," who is without any preferences or concepts of good or bad, so there is nothing to accept or reject. In the past some Dzogchen practitioners did strange things, and people criticized them for their behavior, but Dzogchen Lamas do "crazy" things (by conventional standards) because they have integrated all actions in the state of contemplation and so have no limitations. People criticized them for getting married or eating meat, but they answered that even their way of going to the toilet was not like other people's.

"Crazy wisdom" is activity in accordance with the final, absolute view, the ultimate way of perceiving and being, the snowflake dissolving in the ocean, in which we no longer compulsively repeat the same habitual actions but instead act with crazy abandon, renouncing nothing. Nothing can disturb us any longer, everything arises in its own way and is liberated in its own way. If we do something, it is fine; if we do not do it, it is fine. There are no longer any rules to follow. However, we must develop our mind before we reach this stage. It doesn't work to try to behave in this way without previously having attained correct understanding.

The *Zerbu* continues:

> Do anything without any indecision or hesitation.
> Without expectations or doubts
> All actions are completely free.
> Behavior becomes like a peacock's,
> Taking all negative obstacles and appearances as
>   blessings.
> When unhappy, abide completely in unhappiness;
> When happy, abide completely in happiness;
> When ill, abide completely in illness;

> When hungry, abide completely in hunger;
> When afraid, abide completely in fear;
> When you don't like something, abide completely in
>   the state of not liking.
> This is the big wind.
> When vision is an obstacle, be careful;
> When vision becomes your friend, liberate yourself.
> Then everything becomes a benefit to your practice.

Another text, the *Six Instructions*, says: "Those who practice the five poisons are the best practitioners," because instead of being an obstacle, the energy of the passions becomes a benefit to the practice.

> When you act according to crazy wisdom,
> You are a real vessel of the Dzogchen teaching.
> This is arriving in the gold dimension.

In this dimension everything is gold; there is nothing that is not the pure and perfect state. If everything is gold, then nothing is more valuable than anything else; there is nothing to assign any particular worth to, because everything is precious. There is nothing to hide secretly in your house, and there are no activities to accept or reject. This is the ultimate way to relate with energy in terms of the variety of experience.

13

Öd-nga
The Five Pure Lights

From the five pure lights of the natural mind arise
The unchanging dimension of the body,
The unceasing pure manifestation of speech,
And the undiluted enlightened mind.

The Clear Light

The pure state of the mind, the base of Buddhahood, has a quality of clear light, which develops into the pure light of the natural state. This light is "rainbow light," not material light. It is the natural energy of the primordial state and the cause of samsara and nirvana. Through the movement of this pure light, which is the inner *rigpa* energy in the dimension of the primordial base, the five pure lights develop and begin to appear. This process is represented by the five-colored *tiglé* that surrounds the white *A* and which symbolizes the primordial natural condition.

The pure lights of the five colors constitute the second step in the production of existence; they are the source of the five elements that are the underlying structure of both the external existence of the world and the internal existence of the individual. In seeing these, we perceive the elements in their gross form, but in reality the source of the elements is the pure light of the natural state.

The energy of the five pure lights arises in the primordial base and creates and gives substance to internal and external reality. In the mandala of the human body, this clear light energy resides in the heart, rises through the channels, and is projected through the eyes. It is the basis of all vision and moves from the inner to the outer dimension.

According to the traditional explanation, external existence is constituted by the world in its function of outer mandala or "container" of the individual. The internal existence of the self or individual is divided into internal, external, and secret.

The external existence of the individual consists of the five sense objects perceived by the five sense consciousnesses. Internal existence is the sixth sense consciousness, the mind, together with proprioception or the inner consciousness of the body. Secret existence is the movement of thoughts. In the last analysis, the division of existence into internal and external is based on a false view formed by the conceptual mind regarding the dualistic condition. In the true condition there is no distinction between internal and external since the same empty space gives rise to internal and external existence alike, just as the air inside and outside a jar is the same.

Development of the Five Lights

The five lights can develop in two ways, depending on whether or not one is present in awareness in the primordial state. If there is understanding, the five pure lights give rise to the five pure visions, and wisdom begins to develop the pure body. In this way, the five pure lights give rise to the five pure elements, which give rise to the five internal elements, then successively to the five external elements, the five sense consciousnesses, the five sense organs, the five sense objects, the five bodies, and the five wisdoms. This process leads to nirvana or final, total realization. But if there is distraction and lack of understanding, the five pure lights become gross and start to transform into the five coarse elements, then successively into the five impure organs, five deluded sense consciousnesses, the five deluded sense organs and so on, finally giving rise to the five poisons or five passions, the five negative actions, and the illnesses derived from these. Each passion is connected with the light of a particular color and element. This is the process of continuous transmigration in samsara.

Two Dzogchen Teachings on the Five Lights

In the *Zhang Zhung Nyan Gyud* there are two teachings, about the five pure lights which approach them in slightly different ways. One is found in the "Union of the Four *Chakras*" and the other in the "Mirror of the Luminous Mind."

The "Union of the Four Chakras"

In this teaching, the first *chakra* is the *chakra*, or wheel, of the primordial base. Unless we understand the *chakra* of the primordial base, we cannot understand how the three dimensions of realization (*kayas*) are perfected in the primordial base and so cannot obtain realization. The second *chakra* is the wheel of realization and illusion. Unless we understand this *chakra*, we cannot realize how samsara and nirvana are perfected in the primordial state, how samsara originates from distraction by delusory thoughts and nirvana arises from correct perception. The third *chakra* is the wheel of the points of the body, veins, channels, and energy centers. Unless we understand how the points in the physical body are related, we cannot obtain realization in this particular body and achieve liberation in this very lifetime. The fourth *chakra* is the wheel of the intermediate state. Unless we understand this, we cannot maintain presence after death and attain realization in the clear light *bardo*.

The *chakra* that concerns us here is the second *chakra*, and how the process that leads to nirvana develops through understanding the five pure lights, just as the process of samsara develops through not understanding them. This *chakra* is also associated with an explanation of how existence is derived from the five pure lights.

The Five Wisdoms and Non-obscurations

In the process of nirvana, the emptiness of the primordial state gives rise to the five pure lights; each light is the pure energy source of an element. These five essential lights give rise to the five elemental clear wisdoms: the white pure light, to the wisdom of emptiness associated with the space element; the green pure light, to the wisdom of equanimity or identity associated with the air element; the red pure light, to the discriminating wisdom associated with the fire element; the blue pure light, to the activity wisdom associated with the water element; the yellow pure light, to the mirror-like wisdom associated with the earth element. These wisdoms are the clear lights of the five families of the Sambhogakaya. In their pure form, the five elements are the cause of the pure Sambhogakaya body or dimension; in their impure form, they constitute our physical body and material dimension.

All the elements are based on the space element, and each element contains within itself the spaces of all the other elements. These spaces are connected with the five *dakinis*, or goddesses, of the five elements: the *dakini* of space, the *dakini* of wind (or air), the *dakini* of fire, the *dakini* of water, and the *dakini* of earth.

The five pure lights have the quality of non-obscuration. The luminous white pure light has the positive quality of non-obscuration of benefit; the luminous red pure light has the quality of non-obscuration of the result; the luminous yellow pure light has the stable positive quality of immutability; the luminous green pure light has the positive quality of unobscured affirmative actions.

The Five Pure Lights and the Body

The five pure lights give rise to the five inner elements that are the fundamental base of existence of the body in the pure state. The white pure light of the space element gives rise to the mind and the heart channels; the green pure light of the air element gives rise to the inner wind or breath; the red pure light of the fire element gives rise to the body heat; the blue pure light of the water element gives rise to the circulation of the blood; the yellow pure light of the earth element gives rise to the body flesh. The five pure lights are connected with the inner (mind and heart) and outer space element, the inner (breath) and outer air element, the inner (body heat) and outer fire element, the inner (body liquid) and outer water element, and the inner (body flesh) and outer earth element.

The life process begins from the heart, which is connected with the space element, and develops through the air, fire, water, and earth elements. In this way, the gross material substance of the body originates from the five pure lights. When the death process begins, the process is reversed in the sense that the bodily functions connected with the five elements start to dissolve. The earth element dissolves or "rolls back" into the water element, the water element dissolves into the fire element, the fire element dissolves into the air element, the air element dissolves into the space element. In ordinary beings this is only an energy process of the element functions, but in advanced Dzogchen practitioners this process also takes place physically, so that at death the adept achieves the light or rainbow body, and the material body dissolves into light and leaves no mortal remains except for the hair and fingernails. This is explained in the so-called "Book of The Dead" literature of the Bon tradition and in detail in the chapter in this book on the *bardo*.

In terms of the generation of the physical body, the five pure lights give rise to the five "branches" of the body. From the white pure light arises the head, the branch of the space element; from the green pure light arises the right leg, the branch of the air element; from the red pure light arises the right arm, the branch of the fire element; from the blue pure light arises the left leg, the branch of the water element; from the yellow pure light arises the left arm, the branch of the earth element. The five pure lights also give rise to the five subsidiary branches, which are, respectively, the eyebrows, beard, pubic hair, hair on the head, and hair on the chest.

The five pure lights give rise to the five sense consciousnesses and the five sense organs. From the white pure light arises the distinguishing consciousness of the mind connected with the sense of sight and the eyes; from the green pure light arises the sense of smell and the nose; from the red pure light arises the sense of taste and the tongue; from the blue pure light arises the sense of hearing and the ears; from the yellow pure light arises the sense of touch and the body surface.

The non-obscuration of the five pure lights gives rise to the wisdoms of the five sense consciousnesses. From the white pure light arises the wisdom of the eye sense consciousness; from the green pure light arises the wisdom of the nose sense consciousness; from the red pure light arises the wisdom of the tongue sense consciousness; from the blue pure light arises the wisdom of the ear sense consciousness; from the yellow pure light arises the wisdom of the body (touch) sense consciousness.

The pure five lights are also related to the five sense objects. The white pure light gives rise to form, the object of the sense of sight; the green pure light gives rise to odor, the object of the sense of smell; the red pure light gives rise to flavor, the object of the sense of taste; the blue pure light gives rise to sound, the object of the sense of hearing; the yellow pure light gives rise to tactile sensation, the object of the sense of touch. (Realized beings in addition have the wisdom of synaesthesia, the power to use the senses to contact sense objects that do not correspond to the sense subjects. For example, they can see with their ears, listen with their mouths, and so forth.)

The five pure lights also give rise to the five inner organs. The white pure light of the space element gives rise to the heart; the green pure light of the air element gives rise to the lungs; the red pure light of the fire element gives rise to the liver; the blue pure light of the water element gives rise to the kidneys; the yellow pure light gives rise to the spleen. The five pure lights also give rise to the five impurities or hollow organs, respectively the stomach, large intestine, gall bladder, bladder, and small intestine.

The Five Deities, Powers, Results and Mandalas

From the five pure lights arise the five deities of the center and four directions of the mandala. From the white pure light arises the deity Shenlha Okar at the center of the mandala; from the green pure light arises the deity of the north; from the red pure light arises the deity of the west; from the blue pure light arises the deity of the south; from the yellow pure light arises the deity of the east.

The five classes of deities arise from the five pure lights. From the white pure light arises the natural class of deities; from the green pure light arises the vajra class of deities; from the red pure light arises the lotus class of deities; from the blue pure light arises the jewel class of deities; from the yellow pure light arises the *vishvavajra* class of deities.

The five pure lights give rise to the five great powers or energies. The white pure light gives rise to the power of compassion; the green pure light gives rise to the power of peace; the red pure light gives rise to the power of depth; the blue pure light gives rise to the power of generosity; the yellow pure light gives rise to the power of wisdom.

The five pure lights give rise to the five results or great effects: the white pure light gives rise to the undeluded mind; the green pure light gives rise to the arising of pure qualities; the red pure light gives rise to the non-obscuration of positive qualities; the blue pure light gives rise to effortless perfection that is tied to action; and the yellow pure light gives rise to the condition of immutability.

The five pure lights give rise to the five mandalas of The Great Perfection. The white pure light gives rise to The Great Perfection mandala of space that clarifies existence and makes being possible. Without this space, the structure of phenomenal existence could not arise. The green pure light gives rise to The Great Perfection mandala of air or wind, which enables standing upright without falling down. The red pure light gives rise to The Great Perfection mandala of the energy of fire and brilliancy. The blue pure light gives rise to The Great Perfection mandala of the secondary cause of growth which is like a medicine that gives back health to a dying person. The yellow pure light gives rise to The Great Perfection mandala of the primary cause of growth.

Nirvana and Samsara

This analysis of the evolution of existence from the five pure colors is analogous to the traditional symbolic figure known as "The Wheel of Realization and Illusion." The formation of the five pure elements, the five inner organs, the five wisdoms, and so forth, as presented in that figure, presupposes pure perception and understanding, and the concomitant development of the process of nirvanic liberation. In the case of illusory perception, the five pure lights deteriorate into the five gross elements that degenerate into the five poisons or passions, the five illnesses, etc., and give rise to the whole process of samsaric transmigration.

TABLE OF CORRESPONDENCE
Union of the Four Chakras and Mirror of the Luminous Mind

LIGHTS	PASSIONS	INNER ELEMENTS	LOCATIONS	DOORS	PATHS OR CHANNELS	SUBSIDARY CHANNELS	IMPURITIES (HOLLOW ORGANS)	SENSE INDEX
white	anger	bone	heart	eyes	the channel of the heart is the eyes	eyebrows	right arm	visible objects
green	pride	breath	lungs	nose	the channel of the lung is the nose	beard	left arm	odors
red	desire	heat	liver	tongue	the channel of the liver is the tongue	pubic hair	left leg	tastes
blue	jealousy	blood	kidneys	ear	the channel of the kidneys is the ears	hair of head	head	sounds
yellow	ingorance	flesh	spleen	lips	the channel of the spleen is the lips	hair on chest	right leg	tangible objects

LIGHTS	BIRTH	LOKAS	PURE DIVINITIES	DEMONS	ACTION DEITIES	KAYAS
white	miraculous birth	hell	Kun-nang Cha-ba	demon of illusion	peaceful divinities	Dharmakaya
green	birth from an egg	semigods	Ge-lha Gar-cug	demon of the aggregates		
red	birth from heat	hungry ghosts	Che-drang Ngö-med	demon of delusions	dominating divinities	Sambhogakaya
blue	birth from moisture	animals	Ga-wa Don-drup	demon of ignorance	wrathful divinities	Nirmnakaya
yellow	birth from the womb	human	Sal-wa Rang-jung	demon of death	enriching divinities	

The Process of Samsara

Distraction by delusory thought leads us to misconstrue the nature of the five lights and thus not understand that the five elements are the energy manifestations of our own primordial state. Thus when we see the manifestations of the elements, such as the three great visions that arise in the *bardo*, we misunderstand them and erroneously follow them as if they were external.

The process of illusory misunderstanding mirrors, in a distorted way, the process of evolution of the elements given above, so I will not repeat it at length. The correspondences of the colors with the five lights, the elements, sense consciousnesses, etc., concur with those in pure perception.

The explanations of the correspondences between the colors of the five pure lights and the five passions and realms of existence are far clearer in the *The Mirror of the Luminous Mind*, so I will give them later in this chapter.

The Mirror of the Luminous Mind

When Nangzher Lodpo asked Tapihritsa about the cause of samsara and nirvana, Tapihritsa answered, "The cause of samsara and nirvana is the great base (or primordial state)." *The Mirror of Luminous Mind*, which also explains how to remain in the state of contemplation, is the continuation of Tapihritsa's answer:

> From the energy (*gdangs*) of the emptiness of the primordial state arises the presence or clarity (*gsal ba*) that gives rise to the five lights.

If the nature of the five lights is perceived in pure perception, they give rise to the five pure elements and the process culminating in nirvana takes place.

In the case of the production of samsara, through delusion we do not understand the elements as manifestations of the pure lights of our primordial state, and we perceive them impurely as external and imperfect. The difference between nirvana and samsara, between liberation and illusion, lies precisely in the difference between understanding and delusion, between the presence or absence of the realization of our true condition.

The text gives a detailed explanation of how the movement of the radiant energy arouses the karmic *prana* of movement, giving rise to the consciousness of the conceptual mind. The *"prana* of increase" and the *"prana* of churning" produce the "sound like light" that is the base of the three great visions. When there is misunderstanding of the origin of the five pure lights, they materialize through these movements into the five gross elements and become the cause of all our defilements, the five passions, the five illnesses, and so forth.

The five pure lights are connected with the five passions. When there is delusion regarding the lights, they manifest as the five passions instead of the five wisdoms. The white light is connected with anger, the green light with pride, the red light with desire, the blue light with jealousy, and the yellow light with ignorance.

The inner element corresponding to the white light is the mind (or bone); the breath corresponds with the green light; the body heat with the red light; the blood with the blue light; the flesh of the body with the yellow light.

The five lights pass from their locations within the body, moving through channels and out of the sense organs to connect with their respective sense objects. The white light is located in the heart and passes through the channel connecting with the eyes (as its "door") to visible objects; the green light is located in the lungs and passes through the channel connecting with the nose to odors; the red light is located in the liver and passes through the channel connecting with the tongue to tastes; the blue light is located in the kidneys and passes through the channel connecting with the ears to sounds; the yellow light is located in the spleen and passes through the channel connecting with the lips to tangible objects.

The correspondences for the branches or limbs of the lights are: the right arm for the white light; the left arm for the green light; the left leg for the red light; the head for the blue light; the right leg for the yellow light.

The subsidiary branch of the white light is the eyebrows; that of the green light is the beard; that of the red light is the pubic hair; that of the blue light is the hair on the head; and that of the yellow light is the hair on the chest.

The five lights correspond to the following impure or hollow organs: the white light corresponds to the stomach; the green light to the large intestine; the red light to the gall bladder; the blue light to the bladder; the yellow light to the small intestine.

The text then explains in detail the correspondences between the lights and the types of birth that are possible for sentient beings. The white light leads to miraculous birth; the green light to birth from an egg; the red light to birth from heat; the blue light to birth from moisture; the yellow light to birth from the womb.

The five lights give rise to rebirth in different *lokas*, or dimensions of existence. The white light causes rebirth in hell, the green light rebirth in the realm of the demigods, the red light to rebirth in the realm of the hungry ghosts, or *pretas*, the blue light to rebirth as an animal, the yellow light to rebirth as a human.

The five lights correspond to the following pure deities: the white light corresponds to Kun-nang Cha-ba; the green light to Ge-lha Gar-cug; the red light to Che-drang Ngö-med; the blue light to Ga-wa Don-drup; and the yellow light to Sal-wa Rang-jung; and to the following demons: the white light corresponds to the Demon of Illusion; the green light to the Demon of the Aggregates; the red light to the Demon of Delusions; the blue light to the Demon of Ignorance; the yellow light to the Demon of Death.

There are groups of action deities corresponding to the five lights. The peaceful deities in the east who overcome illnesses and provocations by the *gdon* correspond to the white light, the dominating deities in the west who control the power of gods, demons, and humans that can cause problems, to the red light; the wrathful deities, who cannot be controlled by the dominating deities, to the blue light; the enriching deities, who enhance life and spiritual practice, to the yellow light.

The white light corresponds to the Dharmakaya; the red light, to the Sambhogakaya; the blue light, to the Nirmanakaya.

From this analysis we can see that the whole of internal existence in the mandala of the body and of external existence in the mandala of the universe are derived from the five elements, the material form of the five pure lights. The pure lights are the energy of the empty space of the primordial state that is beyond samsara and nirvana.

14

Trikaya
The Three Dimensions

The empty essence of mind is Dharmakaya;
The clear nature of mind is Sambhogakaya;
The non-duality of mind is Nirmanakaya;

The Trikaya Principle

According to the Bon teachings, the bodies, or dimensions (Sanskrit *trikaya*), are Buddhahood itself. The three bodies are the Dharmakaya, which the Bon tradition translates into Tibetan as *bon sku*, the Body of Bon; the Sambhogakaya (*rdzogs sku*), the Body of Perfection; and the Nirmanakaya (*sprul sku*), the Body of Emanation or Manifestation. I will refer to them by their Sanskrit names with which readers are probably more familiar. The Dharmakaya is the emptiness of the natural state of reality; the Sambhogakaya is the clarity of the natural state; the Nirmanakaya is the movement of energy that arises from the inseparability of emptiness and clarity.

Emptiness is the essence of all existence; this is the *kunzhi* base, the pure presence of clarity in the empty, formless base. Its potential quality of uninterrupted manifestation is the Sambhogakaya; the inseparable state of formless space and clear presence gives rise to the uninterrupted manifestation that is the Nirmanakaya. However, each of the three *kayas* contains the aspects of the other *kayas*, so that emptiness has the aspects of clarity and movement, clarity has the aspects of emptiness and movement, and movement has the aspects of emptiness and clarity.

The dimension or "castle" of the Dharmakaya is the all-pervading base where primordial awareness is spontaneously self-perfected. According to an explanation that is unique to the *Zhang Zhung Nyan Gyud*, in the heart there is pure emptiness, which is the Dharmakaya; this generates light which is the Sambhogakaya and this light is communicated to the eyes; the inseparability of the emptiness in the heart and the light generated in the heart is the Nirmanakaya, the dimension of manifestation, so that the light projected through the eyes (and the other senses) manifests as the three great visions, the sound, light, and rays. In fact, the sound, light, and rays are perfected as the three *kayas*.

The Dharmakaya is the spontaneously self-perfected primordial awareness that resides in the empty space element in the heart. The Sambhogakaya is the potential quality of manifestation of movement of the sound, light, and rays spontaneously perfected in the empty space of the heart. There is a tendency towards dualism here and the Sambhogakaya is connected with individual reality. Another image from the *Zhang Zhung Nyan Gyud* is of a red stone covered by a crystal. The red stone stands for the heart and the crystal for the flesh and fat of the human body. This indicates that the light resides in the physical heart, as explained in the "Five Lights." The Nirmanakaya is located in the three channels and the six *chakras* and, through the potential quality of movement, manifests externally through the five senses. The traditional symbol for individual realization is butter, which is latent in milk but which has to be churned in order to manifest. The nature of milk is the Dharmakaya, its potential for becoming butter is the Sambhogakaya, and the manifestation of the butter is the Nirmanakaya. Or, to use another analogy, we could say that space is the Dharmakaya, my hand is the Sambhogakaya, and the movement of my hand in space is the Nirmanakaya. If there were no space, there could be no hand, and if there were no hand, there could be no movement. Or again, the nature of an object such as a microphone is the Dharmakaya of the microphone, the material microphone itself is the Sambhogakaya, and its function is the Nirmanakaya. Thus it is important to understand that space has this potential quality to manifest the movement of the light, rays, and sound. According to Dzogchen, this movement is not created by the individual mind but is discovered and developed by it, and that it is through the development of this potentiality that realization is ultimately possible.

The omnipervasive Dharmakaya, the primordially empty natural state, is without dualism, like the *chab rig*, the pervading awareness imbuing all existence; when it is connected with the individual dimension, it is Sambhogakaya; when these two are combined, when the primordial awareness resides in a physical body, it is the Nirmanakaya. In fact, without a body, there could only be Dharmakaya and hence no Sambhogakaya or Nirmanakaya.

The Dharmakaya Buddha Kuntuzangpo represents the *kunzhi*, the base of everything. In that empty, formless space, there is the pure, clear presence that is the Sambhogakaya. In the inseparability of formless empty space and clear presence, movement arises. This is the Nirmanakaya. All existence, in the form of the three great visions, derives from the movement of energy in the Nirmanakaya dimension.

Tsal and the Trikaya

The three great visions or movements of energy can also be related to the trikaya principle within the individual. The Dharmakaya is the empty formless space that is the natural state of the mind without thoughts, the *kunzhi* or base of everything. The Sambhogakaya is the clear, spontaneous presence of *rigpa* in the empty, natural state of the mind, and the Nirmanakaya is the inseparability of formless empty space and clarity. This inseparability gives rise to the movement of energy in the form of thoughts. In the intermediate *bardo* state too, all the movements of mind arise in the form of the three great visions. Perceiving that these are our own manifestation is understanding and leads to nirvana; not perceiving it is delusion and leads back to samsara.

The Trikaya in the Individual

The three *kayas* are inherent in the self. They are self-perfected within our own nature they are not extraneous to us. In the physical body, the existence of the three channels and the six *chakras* as the base is the Dharmakaya. The actual channels and *chakras* are the Sambhogakaya and their functional manifestation is the Nirmanakaya. The primordially self-perfected and baseless self-presence is the Dharmakaya. The appearance of images (for example, during dark retreat) due to the relationship of body and mind is the Sambhogakaya, and the appearance of one's visualized body and all the actions performed through the visualization are the Nirmanakaya.

The three *kayas* are spontaneously self-perfected in the pure primordial state of the mind; they are already perfect in our own nature.

The three *kayas* can also be applied to the individual according to two other schemas. In the first, the *kayas* characterize the aspects of base, path, and result of the individual's work as a practitioner.

The Dharmakaya of the base is the principle of emptiness. The Sambhogakaya of the base is the principle of clarity or all-pervading awareness. The Nirmanakaya of the base is compassionate energy, the potentiality for manifestation that follows from emptiness and all pervading clarity's not being separate.

The Dharmakaya of the path is the process of development of the three *kayas* in actual practice on the path. The Sambhogakaya is the experience of the clarity that develops during that process. It is awareness in actual experiential events.

The Dharmakaya of the result is the actual condition of realization.

In the second schema, the three *kayas* are subdivided by themselves, so that we have three triplicities:

First Triplicity:

The emptiness of emptiness, or Dharmakaya of the Dharmakaya;

The clarity of emptiness, or Sambhogakaya of the Dharmakaya;

The energy of emptiness, or Nirmanakaya of the Dharma-kaya.

Second Triplicity:

The emptiness of clarity, or Dharmakaya of the Sambhoga-kaya;

The clarity of clarity, or Sambhogakaya of the Sambhogakaya;

The energy of clarity, or Nirmanakaya of the Sambhogakaya.

Third Triplicity:

The emptiness of energy or Dharmakaya of the Nirmana-kaya;

The clarity of energy or Sambhogakaya of the Nirmanakaya;

The energy of energy or Nirmanakaya of the Nirmanakaya.

In the first triplicity, the emptiness, clarity, and energy remain unsullied by experiences of any kind. They are what they are primordially and eternally. Emptiness remains empty even as it is inseparable from clarity and even as this inseparability is the potentiality for energetic manifestation.

In the second triplicity, we are concerned with appearances. The emptiness of clarity is the emptiness that is the essential nature of all appearances. The clarity of clarity is the appearances themselves. The energy of clarity is the actual events that follow upon the manifestation of the appearances.

In the third triplicity, we are concerned with concrete events and manifestations. This is best understood through an example such as the passion of anger. The emptiness of energy with respect to anger would be the essential emptiness or illusory nature of the anger, the fact that each passion is fundamentally empty and is not in reality as it presents itself to be. The clarity of energy in respect to anger is the manifesting anger itself, the anger that manifests as the appearance of anger. The energy of energy in respect to anger is the action that results from the anger.

Base Buddha, Path Buddha, and Result Buddha

Dzogchen teachings also explain the base Buddha, the path Buddha, the result Buddha or primordial Buddha, manifest Buddha, and perfection Buddha.

The base (or "base enlightened") Buddha is the primordial awareness or self-perfected inner wisdom in the heart. Actually, whether we discover the primordial state in ourselves or not, it is always there: it is inherent in all existence. The primordial wisdom in the heart has the potential quality to manifest sound, light, rays, bliss, and the awakened state. When the primordial awareness that opens all the doors of realization awakens, we start to "see" in a different way. The *rigpa* wisdom that appears from the channels and *chakras* through the eyes, which are the doors of light, is the path or manifest Buddha when we discover and practice it. It is the perfection Buddha when we realize it, when our eyes (and all our senses) are open and we integrate with whatever arises, understanding that everything is the manifest Buddha, regardless of whether what appears is a Buddha or an animal. To integrate wisdom with vision and the other senses completely and never to return to illusion is the perfection Buddha.

In terms of their physical location, the primordial awareness in the heart is the primordial Buddha; the doors of potential awakening in the channels connected with the heart are the perfection Buddha; their manifestation outside these doors is the manifest Buddha.

Dharmakaya	Base Buddha	Primordial Buddha
Sambhogakaya	Path Buddha	Manifest Buddha
Nirmanakaya	Result Buddha	Perfection Buddha

We fully understand the perfection of the three *kayas* when we achieve final realization. This is the final result or effect of meditation practice. A transformation takes place such that the normal physical body of flesh and blood is transformed into the pure body, and the mind that produces thoughts is transformed into nonconceptual wisdom. At this stage the Dharmakaya is explained as emptiness, the Sambhogakaya as the inner manifestation of energy in the form of light, and the Nirmanakaya as the outer manifestation of energy.

Trikaya in Sutra, Tantra, and Dzogchen

The formless, the forms, and the movements or manifestations of forms are the basic principles underlying Sutra, Tantra, and Dzogchen.

According to the Sutra system, the formless state is the absolute truth, the Dharmakaya. It is only after realization that states of form can be understood in terms of absolute truth. The recognition that the three *kayas* are already spontaneously perfected within our own nature is lacking.

In Tantra, the empty self is the Dharmakaya, the deity appearing in oneself is the Sambhogakaya, and the inseparability of oneself and the deity is the Nirmanakaya.

In Dzogchen, realization means understanding that the mind is Buddha. The empty nature of mind is Dharmakaya, the clarity of mind is Sambhogakaya, and all the manifestations of mind (including the passions) are Nirmanakaya. The Dharmakaya, the formless base of everything, the absolute truth, the absolute condition, is depicted by Kuntuzangpo naked with no adornments. The Sambhogakaya is Shenlha Okar, adorned with jewel ornaments, representing clear presence in the formless state. The nirmanakaya is Tapihritsa, the human manifestation arising from the union of clarity and space.

It is important to realize that paying homage to Kuntuzangpo by offering incense and so forth only makes sense if we recognize that his nakedness depicts our own formless state that we project into the representation.

When we practice, the emptiness we discover within the mind, within ourselves, is the Dharmakaya; the subtle existence of clarity, self-understanding, is the Sambhogakaya; and whatever concepts, memories, or passions manifest are the Nirmanakaya.

The Passions and the Trikaya

The figure of the "Wheel of the Primordial Base" explains a practical method to experience the perfection of the three *kayas* in the *kunzhi* base through the passions.

When we sit in meditation, we build up a passion such as anger and then observe the anger when it arises in the mind. We look at it directly and see that it disappears. We cannot say that it disappears into itself; rather, it disappears the same way it arises. The state where it disappears, where it self-liberates, is the pure state of anger. In this way we see that the inherent quality of each energy movement in the mind, each passion as well as each thought, is purity. If we remain in the state where the anger disappears, what we find is that we don't find the anger. We can use the same Tibetan example of losing a yak and going out to look for it and not finding it. Not finding the yak is what we find. In the same way, we try to build up anger, then instead of increasing or developing it, we observe it to see its quality. Thus we find that the natural state of anger is emptiness. We can apply this to every thought and every passion that arises; they all function in this same way.

All the manifestations of the passions are Nirmanakaya and in the Nirmanakaya all existence is derived from the movement of energy in the state of the inseparability of emptiness and clarity, Dharmakaya and Sambhogakaya.

Observing the mind, we can see that all mental movements, all passions and thoughts, contain within themselves the qualities or aspects of the three *kayas*. The Tantras say that anger, in the form of the deity of anger, is the antidote to anger. This means that observing anger and seeing its inherent emptiness is the antidote to anger. This means experiencing its presence and the inseparability of presence and emptiness.

In Dzogchen we do not use an antidote but rather try to understand the aspects of the three *kayas* in each movement of the mind: when we observe a passion dissolve into the pure state, that is the Dharmakaya of the passion, the potential base of the passion. Its clear presence in the pure state of emptiness is the Sambhogakaya of the passion, which is the potential quality of the passion. The inseparability of the clarity of the passion and the empty state in which it is based is the Nirmanakaya of the passion, the actual manifestation of the passion. In practical terms this means that when anger arises, we can see the anger in ourselves, but when we try to examine it closely, we only find the inherent emptiness of anger, the Dharmakaya of anger. In that state of emptiness there is a presence that is the Sambhogakaya of anger, and the inseparability of the anger's emptiness and clear presence is the Nirmanakaya of anger. To be able to find the three *kayas* in all inner and outer appearances as manifestations of our inherent energy, in the mind and in the outer world, is to discover that everything is Buddha.

15

Trekchö and Tögel

This Great Completeness, distillation of the essence,
Is not ascertained as one, it is many.
Not being many, it dwells as one.
The separation of one and many does not exist.
Even its nonexistence is beyond saying "nonexistence."
And this very convention of saying "beyond"
Was never mentioned by Shenrab.

Many of the Dzogchen teachings of the *Zhang Zhung Nyan Gyud* are concerned with light. Dzogchen is a direct path, and the more advanced practices focus on the two methods of *trekchö* (*mkhregs chod*) and *tögel* (*rthod rgal*), which are unique to Dzogchen. *Trekchö* means "cutting loose." It is the practice of single pointed contemplation and consists in remaining in the natural state. *Tögel* means "working" or exerting oneself for direct realization. We do not just remain in the state of contemplation but work on integrating contemplation with the movement of energy in the form of light and vision. Fundamentally this involves the contemplation of light. This work with light and vision proves especially useful in the *bardo* when the three great visions arise. Through such practice we can understand the differences and connections between the subtle dimension and its solid physical representation, our karmic vision.

Practical Advice on Trekchö and Tögel

Remaining in the state of contemplation, abiding in the natural essence of the pure state of mind, is *trekchö*. It is very important to make *trekchö* stable before embarking on *tögel* practice because otherwise our contemplation will not be strong enough for us to be able to integrate it with vision when it arises in order to develop *tögel*.

Many masters say that the *tögel* practices are difficult to apply, but certainly it is useful to receive teachings on *tögel* even if we are not yet able to practice them. Though it is true that it takes a long time to make our contemplation stable through the practice of *trekchö*, this should not become an obstacle for starting to practice *tögel*, otherwise we might find we reach the end of our life without having done *tögel* practice.

The teachings on these types of practices were kept very secret by all the masters of the lineage, from Shenrab Miwoche to the masters of the recent past, many of whom realized the rainbow body. My master, who revealed these teachings to me, emphasized their great importance but also pointed out that although it was correct to keep these teachings secret in ancient times, which were a golden period, they should no longer be kept secret in a time like ours, so full of problems and difficulties, otherwise there is the risk that the lineage of these teachings might come to an end.

Tögel

Tögel teachings in the *Zhang Zhung Nyan Gyud* describe the clear light and naturally arising visions, as well as how these arise and how these are brought into the path. These visions, which are of luminous points or seeds of light and of webs of light in configurations of Buddhas, mandalas and so forth, are formed from the inherent structure of light, the energy expression of the clarity of the primordial state. Specific *tögel* practices include the dark retreat in which we spend time practicing in complete darkness (the

standard dark retreat lasts forty-nine days, although some Dzogchen practitioners have spent many years in dark retreat), or gazing at the sun, at the moon, or into the sky. All these techniques are
used to make it possible for visions spontaneously to arise from
the recesses within our mind. We then work with these.

Five gazes are used to enhance vision in *tögel* practice:

1. the wrathful gaze, with the eyes turned upwards, is useful if we are feeling drowsy;
2. the peaceful gaze, with the eyes turned downwards, is
   useful if our mind is too agitated;
3. the bodhisattva gaze, with the eyes looking straight for-
   ward, is used when the mind is calm;
4. the gaze of method, with the eyes turned to the right,
   develops method; and
5. the gaze of wisdom, with the eyes turned to the left,
   develops wisdom.

Three further types of gaze used in *tögel* practice are: the wheel
gaze; the lion gaze; the secret gaze.

Mandalas, *tiglés* (points of luminous light), white points, circu-
lar rainbows, images of Buddhas, deities, and Buddha dimensions
all may manifest. They are the natural manifestations of our
Sambhogakaya and arise through the wisdom channel that links
our heart with our eyes. When these arise the practice is intermit-
tent, like the sun seen through clouds: at times we are in the state
of presence, at other times we follow the lights. At times it seems
we are practicing, at other times not, so many doubts can arise
that we have to clear up with our master.

In this way we come to experience directly and know the seeds
that are the base or origin of pure visions, which are like the stars
in space. When we start to practice *tögel*, the movement is more
intense. It is like unveiling a multicolored Chinese silk: suddenly
we see many colors in space, like seeing rainbows everywhere.
This is the main vision, the base of five colored lights, from which
all visions arise. This is the importance of the five lights, which
give rise to nirvana and samsara.

Working with the movement of light in *tögel* practice is easier than
working with the solid objects we see and sounds we hear normally

in everyday life, things with which we are already familiar. The *tögel* visions arise as the outer manifestation of inner experiences. There are texts that describe the "movement of the energy of the external light" and the signs that appear during the visions.

Different names are given to the different visions. For example, the "fish of the rays in movement" refers to the movement of the visions and describes visions as moving in the same way a fish moves in waves of water. The text explains that we must try to "catch the fish of the rays in movement in the net of darkness" and describes the "dart" state of presence that we must shoot at the target, which in this case is the fish. Vision is the fish and the dart; the instrument for capturing it is presence.

The Four Tögel Visions

The four stages of *tögel* practice are known as the "four visions of *tögel*." These are:

1. the visionary experience of absolute reality;
2. the increase and intensification of visionary experience;
3. the ripening of *rigpa* awareness to its fullness;
4. the final consummation and exhaustion of phenomena.

The *Zhang Zhung Nyan Gyud* also contains a unique description of the four stages with the phases of the waxing moon in the first half of the lunar month and with the five paths of Sutra training.

Before discussing these four stages it would be useful to look at the four ways visions can arise. The first way is through the self-perfection of the primordial state. This occurs because the visions are inherent in the nature of the primordial state, which is luminosity. The second way is through using skillful methods. These are effective because visions are present in the primordial state in the same way butter exists in milk, and just as we churn the milk to obtain the butter, if we know the right methods, we can draw visions from the state. The third way is the spontaneous arising of visions as a sign of progress in the practice. In this case it is important to distinguish between pure visions and impure visions that can become obstacles to our progress on the path of practice. The fourth way is the spontaneous way visions arise during the *bardo*.

The first of the four stages occurs when vision begins to arise and we have direct insight into the nature of reality. This experience corresponds to realization of the Sutric path of accumulation. The second stage occurs when the arising vision approaches development and we have more experience. This corresponds to the path of endeavour. The third stage is the development and ripening to perfection of awareness of vision and corresponds to the path of seeing and the path of meditation. Finally, the fourth vision, which corresponds to the path of no more training, is the stage of complete vision. Here, on the dissolution of illusory phenomena, we integrate completely with the vision of totality.

More specifically, during the first stage there are two lights, one internal and one external. When we start to practice, we feel as if a light were coming out of us. Here the symbol of the light is the "*tiglé* of the *rigpa* of the color of glass," which means one feels as if one were looking through the bottom of a glass. The *tiglés* are very luminous and can vary in size; the smallest can be the size of a pea, others can be much bigger. Also many *tiglés* can appear joined together in various ways, horizontally, vertically, etc., forming strands or chains, in which case they are called the "thread of compassion" or the "silver thread," as they are white and luminous and resemble silver. The *tiglés* can appear singly or joined together; there are no limits to the possibilities of vision.

When we start to practice, the types of visions that arise also depend on the combination of our personal elements. For some practitioners vision can be predominantly white, for others it can be red, etc. This means that our internal elements are not well balanced. When we are better able to integrate, the elements adjust themselves. We can see for ourselves when the colors of our vision become balanced without one color absolutely predominating; for example, if red had been the only color, now other colors start to appear too. This indicates that our internal elements are becoming balanced and harmonious.

At times the colors appear separately, first red, then blue, white, etc.; at other times symbols appear with visions reflected inside them. Often these visions are fluctuating, like a lightning flash that disappears when we look at it. Sometimes we can see a whole city; sometimes an entire country complete with mountains can appear in a small *tiglé*. But we should not be surprised at this since we can see many big things with our small eyes. At times when we look at the vision that arises, it disappears immediately; or it can remain a very short time and then disappear, like in a video game. It is difficult to define or explain, because we can see many things in many different ways.

This first stage is the foundation, the basis, in which the rays, lights, *tiglés*, and threads of *tiglés* never remain still in one place. They are like a waterfall pouring down from a very high mountain or like drops of quicksilver that are constantly moving. Everything moves at this stage. When the inner movement manifests while we are practicing in the state of presence, we may very well begin by looking in one direction and finish looking in another. This is not like gazing at a still object with the eyes fixed on one point in space as in *zhiné* practice. It is described as being like a mirror and an arrow; when the movement is very fast and difficult to stop, it is difficult to even understand what is moving. At times it seems it is the vision that is moving, at other times we might think it is our eyes, or that the movement is internal, the inner energy of *rigpa*. In fact, in *tögel* everything is connected: external vision, the eyes, and the internal energy, and in the first stage everything moves together. But it is important to understand that once presence is adequately stable we can stop the movement. This is what is described as "catching the fish in the net of darkness," fixing the movement through stable presence.

At this point the presence concentrates in a single point and the inner experience becomes pure and clear, without movement. We remain in the union of emptiness and the clear *rigpa*; the mother and the son are united and happy. This gives rise to a particular joy, and at this point our consideration of having limited sessions of practice finishes so there is no longer any gap between practice and nonpractice. The end of the first stage corresponds to the third or fourth day of the lunar month, when the moon is starting to wax.

At the second stage, vision begins to develop. At first we might see clear light in all directions, see everything as light. Then we start to distinguish the *rigpa tiglés*, as now we have a closer and more precise experience of the elements, even though they are not yet under full control. In the second stage the elements are balanced, so now what appears in the visions is completely different:

we see the five lights, *tiglés*, round rainbows, and lights in the form of tents. The visions are very pure and clear. The silver threads, too, are encircled by the five colors, and syllables, letters, images, and stupas appear within the *tiglés* of awareness. There are all the colors are inside these visions: there is no limit to the arising of vision. In fact, people who have not practiced nor had experience of specific syllables or deities can see images, which are the reflection of their inner vision, that are completely different from those described in the texts.

The best and easiest way to develop these visions is to do a dark retreat, or to practice looking at the rays of the sun (but not directly at the sun) at sunrise or sunset, holding the hands so that the fingers filter the rays of light, to make a connection between the inner light and the outer light. When we observe the outer rays in this way while in the state of presence, these rays act as secondary causes to produce the projections of the inner light onto the palm of the hand. At the beginning we do not see much, but then vision develops and in this way it becomes very easy to see the lights. Other ways are to practice looking, at the rays of light coming through window shutters, or sitting on a mountain and looking at the point where mountain and space meet (this gives rise to what is called "eyebrow" vision). One advantage of the dark retreat is that we can practice without any requirements (such as the rays of the sun) or distractions from the outside world, so it is easier to integrate.

The characteristic of the second stage is that all the visions and movements are more stable. The movement of the "fish" slows down and may even stop completely. This stability is the first sign of development. This is like when the sea becomes calm, no longer ruffled by the wind.

When the movement stops, we must try to concentrate more. This stage is like the fifth and sixth days of the waxing moon when the moon starts to rise. Even though we may not formally be practicing, we are nevertheless still in the practice. We may have the experience of finishing a practice session and finding that we are still continuing to practice.

In the third stage the visions may be stable and still, or they may move. Different syllables or parts of the body may appear and visions of Buddhas and mandalas arise. There is no longer any difference between external visions and internal experiences, subject and object, nirvana and samsara in this empty reality. At this point we are in the eighth and ninth day of the lunar month, about half-way through the phases of the waxing moon.

We started by going beyond the limited sessions of practice; what we must aim to do is to make all moments and events the same in the state of presence. Developing in this way, we find ourselves in presence both within and without the formal practice sessions. This is natural continuation of presence. However, at this stage we have to discard as dualistic even the idea of practice and non-practice. We enter into the meditation of inner space and abandon this subtle dualistic concept.

The development of this stage leads to the perfecting of the visions. The visions of mandalas, pure Buddha realms, the five Dhyani Buddhas, or of other Buddhas arise perfectly and spontaneously, endowed with all the virtuous qualities. All is perfect in the primordial state of the individual; nothing is hidden and everything is manifest. In pure vision all the mandalas of the peaceful and wrathful deities manifest; we see all the principal and secondary deities and their mandalas clearly and precisely adorned with all the ornaments and attributes, uninterruptedly and without limits.

The text explains that the practitioner will see five groups of deities; however, as visions are the externalized manifestation of our natural condition, there are no limits to the types of visions we may have. In fact, the vision in itself is not important: what is important is to integrate it and to realize that the source of the vision is our own primordial state.

At this stage the visions are very stable and still, like a turtle placed in a dish of water that withdraws into its shell and stops moving. They are visions of perfection because they arise perfected from the primordial state. All the external world is seen as light. We can understand how the inherent existence of all external things, such as houses, mountains, etc., is light, and how it is only when we grasp them that they become solid. When we say they exist as light, this means that they are derived from the elements, which originate from light and which solidify into concrete existence. The point is to understand in what way all reality starts from this condition, from light that can transform itself into material objects.

At this stage we also speak of one taste. This means that even the subtle dualistic concept of presence and lack of presence must be abandoned. We must be without any conflict or effort to practice; we must go beyond the concept of practice and practitioner. These concepts are freed in the primordial state and we remain in pure mind without meditation and without distraction. In fact, in Dzogchen the best meditation is "nonmeditation," beyond meditation. We become one with the meditation, so there is no longer any meditator, any meditation, or anything to meditate on. But this does not mean that there is nothing to do and that we should merely go to sleep; it means that what is needed is the effortless spontaneity of remaining in presence in undistracted meditation. If no effort of concentration is required, this means there is no distraction.

At the end of this stage, we are at the thirteenth and fourteenth days of the lunar month. Between these two days, there is still meditation on space. Through integration we initially overcame the dualism between practice and nonpractice; then we also went beyond the subtle dualistic concept of integration, of contemplation and noncontemplation in which to integrate it, to arrive at the spontaneous continuation of the state that is the meditation on space, on nothingness or emptiness, wherein there is no subject or object, no inner or outer. In the final stage, the stage of realization, we must also overcome the concept of presence or meditation itself.

The fourth stage is the final or ultimate vision. Here all the visions of form, of deities and mandalas, vanish. They are inherently empty and they disappear into the emptiness that is their essence, into the *kunzhi*, the primordial state without attributes. When we stop thoughts, everything stops. All concepts, including the concept of meditation, are liberated in the pure state; all the forms and visions we have described which are based on sound, as well as the sound, light, and rays themselves, disappear into the primordial state. All the sounds disappear like an echo; the light disappears like a rainbow vanishing into the sky; all the rays manifesting as forms and bodies disappear like reflections in water. It is difficult to explain how they disappear: it is said to be "like a dumb man's dream." Everything vanishes like the son returning into his mother's lap. This is total self-liberation, where there is no longer even the possibility of concepts. We finally understand there is neither illusion nor liberation and have the real and final comprehension of the original source whence everything comes and where everything returns. All subtle dualistic concepts, including that of meditation and non-meditation, end, and there is emptiness and nothingness, only wisdom. Someone might object that if there is wisdom, there is something; but wisdom is not a concept, it is direct knowledge unmediated by thought, so there is not even any longer the category of something and nothing. We no longer have any expectations or anything to accept or renounce. This stage is like the space in which the elements vanish, the reality of emptiness that is beyond samsara and nirvana.

This is the fifteenth day of the lunar month, the full moon, and we have attained the final stage, the primordial state, the realm of the primordial Buddha, Kuntuzangpo; we are in his citadel. Just as when someone tells a lie, if another person says, "It's a lie," the lie vanishes; in the same way all concepts vanish through this wisdom that understands that they do not exist.

The final result, enlightenment or realization, is nothing other than this. Through this practice we gain real understanding, we no longer have any expectations about deities and so on, and everything vanishes. When we reach this stage there is a transformation, and the physical body is transformed into the pure light body, the mind with all its thoughts is transformed into wisdom, which is without concepts. In this condition the three *kayas* are perfected; the Dharmakaya is emptiness; the Sambhogakaya is light and the internal manifestation of energy; the Nirmanakaya is the external manifestation of the energy. The understanding of the light nature of reality brings about the ultimate fruit of *tögel* practice, the realization of transference into the light body in which the physical matter of the body is transubstantiated and dissolves into its essential state as pure energy in the form of light.

This is the explanation of the skillful *tögel* practice of the Dzogchen path, which can be traversed and accomplished in a single lifetime, "in one skull," or, in the language of Dzogchen, "in one life and one body."

*Lopon Tenzin Namdak Rinpoche
with the author, Dolanji, 1986*

Nangzhig Monastery in Tibet, 1986

Dialectic School of Monks, Dolanji, 1992

The author with his family, Dolanji, 1986

16

Sutra and Dzogchen

Absolute Reality According to Sutra and Dzogchen

The Sutra and Dzogchen approaches differ in how they understand the meaning of absolute reality. According to the Sutra "Middle Way" (Madhyamika) philosophical system, absolute reality is defined as "lacking inherent existence". This lack of inherent existence is itself emptiness. It possesses the quality that in Dzogchen is called primordial purity. According to Dzogchen, absolute reality possesses not only this quality, but also the inseparability of primordial purity and spontaneous, perfect accomplishment: emptiness and clarity, essence and nature.

According to Sutra, absolute reality is defined as having only the quality of emptiness, whereas in Dzogchen absolute reality indicates emptiness inseparably united with clarity. The "lack of inherent existence" is defined as essence (*ngo bo*), the base of everything (*kun gzhi*) or the mother (*ma*). Understanding emptiness alone is not primordial wisdom. In Dzogchen the emphasis is on understanding the inseparability of clarity and emptiness in the primordial state.

In the Sutra system, emphasis is on the unification of the relative and absolute truth. This is one of the most difficult things to comprehend in the Sutra system. It is easier to understand the lack of inherent existence than the relative truth, namely, that there is relative existence. There is the absolute reality of emptiness but there is also the relative reality of subtle relative existence. Although there is existence, if we try to find it we do not find anything; nevertheless, we know that it exists, but this knowing is not like normal knowledge. It is because there is existence as well as nonexistence that Dzogchen speaks of the inseparability of emptiness ("nonexistence") and clarity ("existence") in the natural state.

Ultimate Truth According to Sutra and Dzogchen

The eighth Bon Way, the "Way of the White A", is in agreement with Dzogchen in finding four errors in the Sutra view of ultimate truth.

1. The error of "finalization." According to the Sutra view, the ultimate truth of the lack of inherent existence is a "nonaffirming negation." By "finalizing" the definition of reality by insisting that there is nothing more to say beyond that it is mere emptiness and nonexistence, the Sutra negates the spontaneous perfection and potentiality for wisdom of the absolute.

2. The error of "letting slip." According to the Sutra view, all phenomena lack inherent existence and therefore lack the qualities of potential manifestation and spontaneous perfection. The Sutra practitioner understands reality as only emptiness and lets himself "slip" into mere emptiness.

3. The error of "being nihilistically limited." According to the Sutra view, the nonaffirming negative lacks the recognition of wisdom and of the Sambhohakaya because it does not define itself as spontaneously perfected like space. This limitation of truth to emptiness means that it is "nihilistically limited."

4. The error of being "nihilistic." According to the Sutra view, the correctness of the law of cause and effect's functioning in relative existence is established by the conventional, conceptual, analytic

mind. As the existence of this mind has to be established by the same sort of conceptual mind, this leads to an infinite regress of conceptual minds confirming the existence of conceptual minds. This is the error of "nihilism."

Discovering Emptiness

Although the aim of the Sutra teachings is the same as that of Dzogchen, i.e., to discover the absolute truth, their respective ways of bringing about this discovery differ. When Sutra masters talk about achieving the understanding of emptiness, this understanding is reached through the conceptual mind, through thought. In the Sutra system a practitioner observes an object and tries to understand its empty essence. This understanding arises through the concept of emptiness. Then, with that conceptual understanding, the practitioner tries to penetrate to a direct and nonconceptual understanding of emptiness. In contrast, instead of analyzing an object by means of conceptual thought, Dzogchen uses direct transmission—the direct and immediate introduction to emptiness, together with various forms of *zhiné*—to understand the empty nature of reality and the emptiness aspect of the primordial state.

For example, to understand emptiness, a Sutra practitioner will investigate an object such as a rose in order to examine its inherent emptiness. When he sees the rose, his mind forms a concept, i.e., a mental image of the rose, and he experiences the meaning generality of "rose" and not the real, sensorially perceived rose. He turns from the sense perception to the mental concept of rose, projects the mind-formed meaning generality "rose" onto the actual rose and projects the mind formed meaning generality "emptiness" onto the meaning generality "rose." Then, by logic, he understands the inherent emptiness of the rose. But according to Dzogchen, this understanding by mental concept of the emptiness of the meaning generality is not necessary to experience directly the emptiness of the actual rose itself. Though the goal is direct perception of emptiness, the Sutra practitioner may spend many years knowing only the concept or meaning generality of emptiness, without ever coming to the direct perception and immediate experience. In practice, he places greater emphasis on the concept of emptiness than on the direct experience of emptiness. The adept practices *zhiné* separately while studying to understand emptiness. He wishes to understand both relative and absolute truth through logic and then tries to integrate this understanding with *zhiné* concentration practice. That is, by developing the thought of emptiness, the understanding becomes clearer, until, in the final stage, understanding by clarity without thought is expected to manifest. However, because this understanding is reached through conceptual analysis, there is always a central point from which the analysis starts. This understanding is therefore always linked with conceptual thought. This is not the direct understanding of emptiness found in Dzogchen, achieved directly through practice and unmediated by thought. In fact, according to Dzogchen, the thought "Now I understand emptiness" is not true understanding but just another thought. The direct understanding of emptiness in Dzogchen is without subject or object and without reference to a central point.

The use of the concept of emptiness in the Sutric tradition to gradually lead the practitioner to an experience of emptiness demonstrates the gradual perspective of the Sutra path. Dzogchen, in contrast, is a nongradual path, and from the very beginning the master teaches the practitioner to seek to understand emptiness directly without thought, through *zhiné* practice. Through the application of mind beyond thought and concepts, we achieve undistracted presence and understanding of the inseparability of emptiness and clarity. The understanding of emptiness arises without the mediation of the thought-producing mind but directly by clarity.

This way of coming to knowledge is unique to Dzogchen. Some Sutra practitioners are shocked when we tell them that in Dzogchen the experience of emptiness is immediate, gained by direct perception without using logic. They say that it is not possible. But Dzogchen asserts that there are two different ways of acquiring knowledge, by logic and through experience. According to Dzogchen, the best way of understanding emptiness is not by applying thought, because the understanding obtained in this way can never go beyond the conceptual level. The logical mind comes to understand the logical concept of emptiness, but the truth of emptiness is beyond thought and concept, beyond the logical mind. True emptiness cannot be understood by logical inference because thought, the conceptual mind, can only understand the concept or meaning generality of emptiness and cannot directly perceive emptiness itself.

Who then understands emptiness? There is the self-understanding of emptiness by emptiness itself, by the clarity aspect of emptiness that enables understanding by direct perception. Understanding is not separate from emptiness. Emptiness understands itself and illuminates itself, as in the example of the butter-lamp. Herein lies the inseparability of emptiness and clarity; self-understanding is self-clarity or self-awareness.

17

Bardo
Death and Other Intermediate States

Preparing for Death

The practices we apply during our lifetime help us during the death process and in the *bardo*. For example, if we have a fatal disease and realize we are going to die soon, what is the best thing to do? How should we prepare for the moment of death? In that last moment when our breath stops, we cannot do a practice for long life because our body, speech, and mind become so weak that we can neither think nor act. We need to understand beforehand what is going to happen in these last moments from instant to instant, and remember how to remain in the state of total presence. We need to remember our master, our *yidam* (personal sacred deity) and the teaching on how to remain in total awareness through-out all the suffering of that last moment between life and death. People who have not made a connection with the teachings find the moment of death very difficult to face or even to think about because of their fear of the unknown and because of attachment to people and possessions in life.

People who have not met the teachings often have no idea about the nature of death, about what is likely to happen to them when death comes, or how to prepare for it. When such a person learns that their death is immanent and comes to me in great anxiety and perplexity looking for help, there is little I can do in terms of precise instructions. I can only give some general reassurance. In contrast, people who have heard the teachings about the *bardo* state and have prepared for death accordingly face death with equanimity and composure. In the Bon monastery where I was trained, there was an old monk who found out that he had to die soon. He did not despair. On the contrary, he started to prepare for death by giving away his possessions and getting ready all the things he would need for his funeral, sewing the special clothes, buying wood for the funeral pyre, and so on. But while he was preparing everything, another monk died suddenly, and Lopon Tenzin Namdak asked if the first monk would give his clothes and wood for the other monk's funeral. The monk cheerfully agreed and started again to prepare himself for his own death. On the night when he was to die, he asked Lopon Tenzin Namdak to stay with him, to chant the *bardo* instructions on death. He was ready for his death and faced it without worry or concern, because in his life his practice had prepared him for this great step.

The Analogy Between Death and Sleep

There is an analogy between the death process and falling asleep. Before going to sleep we think, "Now I am falling asleep." This is comparable to learning that we have a fatal illness. Then we slowly fall asleep. This is like the elements "rolling back" into each other during the death process. The first part of our sleep at night is very deep. Before dreams start to arise, our mind is not conscious and there is no kind of awareness. This stage is similar to the mind or consciousness principle returning to the primordial state at the moment of death in the first *bardo*, "the fundamental base *bardo*." While we are dreaming we are not sure whether we are alive or dead, only when we wake up in the morning do we realize that we are alive. Likewise, in the period immediately after death we do not at first understand that we are dead. It is not easy to accept that we have now departed from life. There is clarity in this state, in fact there can be too much clarity, making it difficult to remain present, as when a mirror reflects too much light so that we are unable to see. This is like the "clear light *bardo*." When the clear light arises in the *bardo* it may be too strong and bright.

It is from the empty space of the fundamental base *bardo* that the clear light *bardo* visions arise. In the same way, dreams arise from our mind in sleep. If we are distracted by the contents of a vision so that fear arises, we have problems and the process of samsara starts; but if we recognize the nature of the visions, then we know nothing is going to happen and we are not afraid. We recognize visions as the products of our own mind. We experience the same empty space in sleep and after death. If we understand this, then we are ready for all the lights, sounds, and visions that arise when the process of clarity develops after death.

Dream Practice

It is a good practice to reflect on these things when we are falling asleep and to try not to be distracted by dreams. This means not only that we should try to understand that we are dreaming while we dream, but that we should try to maintain the presence of awareness during the dream. Through dream practice and the natural light practice, we develop presence in the pure natural state of the mind during sleep. If we are able to maintain continuity of presence during our waking hours, we will eventually be able to maintain it through the moment of falling asleep and into our dreams. We can then use this ability to remain aware when we are dreaming to develop other practices, such as tantric transformations. Maintaining the presence of awareness while dreaming is also useful in this way: if we are able to control our mind and our vision of reality in our dreams, then it will become easier to control our mind and our vision of reality in our waking life. In this way we can free our capacity and energy by unblocking the limitations our mind imposes on us.

Our capacity to remain present in dreams anticipates our capacity to remain present in the moment of death and in the *bardo* state. Without having developed the capacity to practice while dreaming or without having accomplished the *zhitro* practices of the peaceful and wrathful deities, it is very difficult to achieve realization in the *bardo*.

The Death Process

The separation between life and death is potentially the boundary between suffering and happiness. It can be the moment of liberation from attachment and from the limitations of this life. The *Zhang Zhung Nyan Gyud bardo* teachings explain that during the death process the five elements dissolve or "roll back" into each other. As the force of each of the elements and its corresponding part of the body weakens, it rolls back into the next element, which then manifests. Thus earth (yellow) rolls into water (blue), water into fire (red), fire into air (green), and ultimately air rolls back into space (white), when the mind and body separate at death. Finally, the space element dissolves into the "*A*," the *kunzhi*, the natural primordial state. This reverses the order in which the elements develop during the formation of the physical body. It is important to explain these teachings to *vajra* brothers and sisters when they are dying, clarifying their doubts and reminding them about the teaching and the practice.

When the death process starts, there are internal and external signs. The first internal sign is that the energy system of the spleen declines, indicating that the earth element is rolling back. The external sign is that our sensations of bodily warmth and vigour diminish. We can no longer raise the left hand, the limb connected with the spleen. Because the body consciousness has stopped functioning, we lose our sense of touch and our ability to control of our movments. We lose power over "the nine apertures," from which impure fluids start to pour. At this stage it is said that the superior practitioner should die in total awareness at the level of the absolute view, "like a snowflake dissolving in the ocean." If we are aware of the whole death process, it will not be an obstacle to our practice, and our understanding of the true condition will give rise to realization. If we are average practitioners, we will not be capable of this, but we can still try to recognize that our spleen is no longer functioning and that our energy is declining, so that this does not become an obstacle to our presence and understanding.

The next element, water, rolls back into fire. There is dysfunction of the kidney energy, we lose our sense of hearing, and our body loses its glow. We cannot move the left leg, the limb connected with the kidneys, and we lose control of the urinary function.

When the fire element rolls back into air, the corresponding organ is the liver. The tongue goes dry and we lose the sense of taste and the sensation of body heat. We cannot move our right hand, and blood comes out of our nose. We begin to feel cold.

Next, the air (or wind) element rolls back into the space element and the lungs, the organ associated with the air element, cease functioning. We lose the sense of smell, the use of the right leg and control of the defecatory function.

When the space element rolls back into the *kunzhi*, the heart, the organ related to the space element, stops functioning, and we lose the sense of sight as the heart is connected with the eyes. Vital fluid comes out of the body. The heart is also connected with the head, so when the heart stops working our head drops. Often when great masters die, the four active elements (earth, water, fire, and wind) go though the normal process, but the space element energy does not stop functioning immediately as it does in ordinary beings, so the heart remains warm for several days after death. For example, when the sixteenth Karmapa died, his heart remained warm for three days. His doctors were very surprised and could not explain what was happening. Often a great master's head remains upright and the body stays in the meditation posture for three days after death. Then it keels over and semen comes out of the body. The space element energy endures in the heart because the master remains in the state of presence.

We can train ourselves to know and remember the death process by visualizing it when we are falling asleep. One way to practice is to imagine the spleen ceasing to work, then the kidneys, the liver, and the lungs.

In terms of the *chakras*, the *chakra* that dissolves when the earth element rolls back into the water element is the navel *chakra*. At this point the body begins to feel heavy. When the death process begins, we can have certain visions or experiences, such as seeing external lights corresponding to the inner elements. When the navel *chakra* dissolves, it is possible to experience the appearance of flashing yellow light. At this point a fellow practitioner should recite the *bardo* prayers to remind the dying person of the true nature of what they are experiencing.

When the water element rolls back into the fire element, the body glow disappears and the secret *chakra* dissolves. We see a flashing blue light. The moisture of the body dries up and the ears and nose become dry.

When the fire element rolls back into the air element, the throat *chakra* dissolves. The dying person sees a flashing red light. The body heat disappears and we start to feel a strange numbing sensation in the tongue, and we can no longer articulate speech.

When the air element rolls back into the space element, the head *chakra* dissolves and we see a flashing green light. The mind sense consciousness dissolves into the *kunzhi* base consciousness when the breath stops. The dissolution of the physical body sense consciousness of a great Dzogchen practitioner into the *kunzhi* produces the rainbow body when the elements progressively roll back into each other and finally dissolve into their essential nature, which is light. The dissolution of the sense consciousness leaves behind the hair and nails, which are the impurities of the body.

The *bardo* process and visions begin when the mind and body separate, and we experience deep, black darkness. We cannot close our eyes, which roll back, and we see a flashing white light. In this moment it is important for our master and fellow practitioners to help us by making noises and shouting out the teachings to awaken our mind.

The death process is not necessarily experienced in the same way by everybody. If we are fortunate and our karma is meritorious, then we may die in a natural way so that we are able to be fully conscious of the death process and able to remember the teachings. But if we die when we are unconscious or during an accident, the progressive rolling back of the elements may not occur in such a regular way and we may not be mindful of it because the whole process gets compressed into a short time, making it more difficult to avoid distraction. We need to understand the death process as it is happening, whether it is long or short. If we cannot be aware of this, then it is necessary to be aware as soon as the *bardo* begins.

The visions we see in the moment of death are often related to those that arise in the intermediate state, so we should integrate these together. For example, if we die in a hospital, we should try to see the doctors and nurses as *bardo* visions, in this way connecting the two visions of life and death.

The Six Clear Knowledges and Six Recollections

After the body and mind have separated at the moment of death, from this moment on, the consciousness principle is without the support of the body and it is difficult not to be distracted by the visions that occur. People without a superior capacity for Dzogchen or higher Tantric practices, who are of average capacity or who only have simpler teachings and practices, should try to apply the Six Clear Knowledges and the Six Recollections. Each clear knowledge and recollection serves also to remind us of the next one. The Six Clear Knowledges are:

1. The knowledge that our life is in the past and that our death is in the present. First we must understand that there has been a transformation and that we are dead, and we must be able to distinguish between death, our present state, and life, our past state. Mindful of the death process, we remember the dissolution of the inner elements and understand that we cannot continue living now that they have ceased to function, so we should not be attached to anything. In particular, we should overcome our inner attachment to the body and our outer attachment to relatives and friends and to the objects and possessions of our past life.

2. The knowledge that, as the base is free of obscurations, the knowledge of cause and effect arises.

3. The knowledge that with the eyes of the deities there is complete knowledge of the pure and impure visions and dimensions.

4. The knowledge that when the three great visions (sound, light, and rays) arise, there is the recognition that we are in the *bardo* of the clear light of the essential reality.

5. The knowledge that these three visions are our own manifestations, and through our master's instructions and introduction to the nature of the mind and of existence there

arises the understanding that the Trikaya exist spontaneously in our mind.

6. The knowledge that through the introduction to the inner vision the three great visions are recognized as the spontaneous manifestation of the Trikaya in our mind.

The Six Recollections are:

1. Our past lives. We remember all the visions and experiences of all our past lives.
2. The *bardo* and its stages. The acknowledgment that we are dead serves to remind us of the *bardo* and its stages.
3. This reminds us that our mind (consciousness principle) is without support.
4. This reminds us of our master and his instructions, especially the master who gave us instructions on the *bardo*. When we remember our master, we should visualize him, with strong devotion, in front of us.
5. This reminds us of his explanation that the three great visions are our own projections, the manifestations of the energy of our own *rigpa*.
6. This reminds us of our master's teaching that the essence of our mind is pure, and we remember our yidam (personal sacred deity) and the practices to perform in the *bardo*. We should visualize ourselves as the deity, recite the deity's heart mantra, and remember all the peaceful and wrathful *zhitro* deities and the way they are related to ourselves. This practice enables us to remain in the state of baseless presence and to liberate our mind into the essential nature of reality.

The Bardo Visions

When vision of the outer elements — the elements of worldly existence — ceases, the three great visions arise. If we recognize that they are the expressions of the energy of our own *rigpa* and that we are in the clear light *bardo*, we can avoid being distracted by the *bardo* visions and being drawn back into transmigration. In the *bardo* it is especially important to remember our master, the teachings we have received, and our practice. That is why a lama once told his attendants that when he was dead, they should shout out his master's name. Of course he knew his master's name, but he wanted to be reminded of it so that he would be sure to remain aware of it.

Immediately after death our mind separates from our body. Depending on its karma, the mind remains near the corpse for two or three days. For this reason the corpse should not be cremated immediately. If we do not have clarity during this phase, our mind may remain near the corpse four or five days without understanding that it is dead or otherwise comprehending what is happening.

If we have practiced the *powa* transference practice, then this is the moment the presence manifests and we transfer our mind from the crown of our head. It is better to do this ourselves, but if we do not have the capacity then the Lama can do it. Here it is important not to be distracted and to unite our mind essence with the master and the three *kayas* visualized above our head. The *powa* practice is important if we are not able to self-liberate immediately. The deceased person's master or another Lama does the *powa* practice once a week for him, feeds his spirit with burnt offerings, and recites the *bardo* prayers for forty-nine days to guide his mind through the *bardo* experiences.

A Bonpo Funeral Rite

There is a special funeral ritual performed by a Bon practitioner for recalling the dead person's *la* (soul, or consciousness principle) and harmonizing his energy. If in life the person had a problem with the functioning of his vital energy, for instance if one has suffered a serious illness, then his "*la* stone," the "soul turquoise" he wears around his neck, is attached to an arrow and put in the right foreleg of a puppet deer placed on a dish floating on a tank of "white water" (water mixed with milk) containing a white stone and a black stone. During the ritual the water is stirred so that the plate moves around, while the officiating lama makes offerings and attempts to summon the person's soul. If the deer is facing the altar when the dish stops moving, it is a sign the ritual has been successful. If it is facing away from the altar towards the entrance to the house, the ritual has been unsuccessful and has to be repeated until the *la* has been recalled.

If the energy dysfunction is caused by illness, then the practitioner has to pull the white stone out of the water. He must repeat this until he is successful. In an alternative ritual system he must play at dice against the animal of his birth year until he wins. In the case of the death ritual, the dead person's *la* turquoise is brought to the lama and placed on a paper tablet with a drawing representing the person and on which his name has been written. Then the places on the body corresponding to the six *lokas* are burnt to eliminate and liberate all negative causes of rebirth. It is also necessary to have the person's *la* stone, or at least his name or some symbolic representation of him, in order to do the *powa* for him.

The Bardos

After death, on the separation of mind and body, the mind consciousness, the perceiver of form and all concepts dissolves into space. The mind becomes naked, and self-awareness becomes clear and unobstructed, free from obscurations. It is at this moment that the mind enters the *bardo*.

Bardo teachings are found in two texts in the *Zhang Zhung Nyan Gyud* cycle: *The Four Chakras*, and *The Instructions on the Six Lights*. Different teachings and traditions list different numbers of *bardo* states. *The Four Chakras* defines three *bardo* states after death:

1. The *bardo* state of the fundamental base;
2. The *bardo* state of the clear light;
3. The *bardo* state of the nature of existence.

A fourth *bardo* is considered to be the state of existence when we return for our next life. According to another system, this *bardo* is the period between birth and the arising of the fatal illness that will cause and lead to our death. The period between the onset of the fatal illness and death itself is the fifth *bardo*.

The Bardo of the Fundamental Base

After the end of the death process, the consciousness principle enters the *bardo* state of the fundamental base. This state is blank and empty. The master introduces the inseparability of the essence and nature to the dead person in that moment. This recognition is our main practice in life and our most helpful friend in this important moment of the death process. In the first instant after death, it is of no consequence whether in life we were a good practitioner and accumulated much merit or were an inferior practitioner and accumulated negativities. At this precise moment, regardless of whether we have accumulated merit or not during our life, we can recognize our essential nature and liberate ourselves from samsara. In fact, if there is no recognition in this moment, even the accumulation of merit cannot help us. Here the Sutra concept of cause and effect no longer obtains. Efforts we made in our past life make no difference. This is the moment to apply the "path of force." If in this moment we have the strong force of our practice, we can quickly gain enlightenment. The mind of every person on dying is pure and clear, and the consciousness principle shoots out from the right eye of males and from the left eye of females. We should try to eject it upwards from the eyes.

The Bardo of the Clear Light

If we are not able to be liberated during the fundamental base *bardo*, our mind proceeds to the *bardo* state of clear light. Here vision arises because of the movement of the energy of *rigpa*. But between the first and second *bardos* we have another chance to liberate our mind, because, just as we experience clarity when we wake from sleep or when we become aware of our samsaric "madness," in this moment everything becomes very clear. Before the clear light *bardo* starts, there is a moment when it is possible to have presence. This moment, however, is short and, though very clear, very difficult to recognize. It is the moment when the son, the *rigpa* awareness, can recognize and be present in the mother, the empty *kunzhi*, and when they can reunite.

The *bardo* prayer says:

May mother and son meet together in the clear light *bardo*.

If the son recognizes the mother in that state, we can liberate ourselves from the limitations of the impure body, voice, and mind. Everything becomes light, the presence of awareness and the empty essence join together like two fires, purifying the body, voice, and mind into the pure body, voice, and mind of enlightenment.

The fundamental base *bardo* is completely blank: we feel we cannot change anything. In the *bardo*, in contrast, there is clarity, so it is easier to work with our mind. The experience is similar to our becoming during a dream. Here, the movement of *rigpa* produces visions, and when the inner elements cease functioning, the colors of the elements start to appear, giving rise to the appearance of the sound, light, and rays. Often in this *bardo* different colors appear on different days: first white, then green, red, blue, and yellow, corresponding to the elements.

The visions that arise in the clear light *bardo* seem to appear externally. However, if the mind understands the origin and nature of the visions; in particular, if it understands that actually there is nothing it can contact externally, and if it realizes that what appears arises within the mind itself, it sees the visions as its own manifestation and so liberates them. In the first moment there may be presence and the mind may recognize that the visions are of its own nature. But if in the second moment the mind is distracted by the visions, then the *rigpa* is disturbed. The self is deluded as to the nature of the visions and becomes attached to them as if they were something external. Then the process of samsara begins. If we realize the source and nature of the visions and integrate them, unifying our presence with the visions, then the process of the pure visions starts. The visions arise as pure, and the process of the pure elements develops all kinds of forms as manifestations of the pure state of the Sambhogakaya in ourselves. If we fail to attain realization during the clear light *bardo*, attaining realization becomes increasingly difficult. In fact, this is the moment when individual samsara (or nirvana) arises: if we have understanding in this moment we are liberated into nirvana; if we are deluded then we return to samsara. The *Zhang Zhung Nyan Gyud* says:

> Here one sees all the dimensions.
> Light is like a rainbow appearing in the sky;
> Sound is like a garuda dragon, like a thunderstorm;
> The rays are like silk of different colors.

Trekchö and Tögel Practice for the Bardo

Trekchö and *tögel* practice correspond to these two *bardos*. In fact, the purpose of *trekchö* and *tögel* practice is to have the possibility of obtaining the rainbow body at the end of this life. If we fail to do this, we may try to achieve realization during the *bardo*. The *bardo* of the fundamental base corresponds to *trekchö* practice. This gives the possibility of integrating presence in the reunion of mother and son. Here we are working with simple presence without vision. The clear light *bardo* corresponds to *tögel* practice in which, as we have discussed, we work with vision. In the *tögel* dark retreat, various lights and visions appear. When these visions arise, we must remain in undistracted presence in the state of contemplation and learn from what we experience so that we can recognize the visions of the clear light *bardo* when they appear there after death. Also, through *tögel* practice we learn to integrate visualized objects with physical objects. If we succeed at this, we can obtain realization before death and obtain the rainbow body by integrating our physical body with the light that is its nature and which we have visualized in our practice.

If we have practiced *tögel* sufficiently, we will be able to identify the visions that arise in the clear light *bardo*, like recognizing an old friend. We can then liberate ourselves by knowing how to integrate these visions in the state of knowledge. All the manifestations of the inner mandalas arise here through the movement of the mind's energy. There are three things that it is important to remember in order to have precise and clear understanding that we are in the *bardo*:

1. To have a thorough experience of the clear light during our lifetime through practice; especially through doing the dark retreat as often as possible.

2. To have a very clear reminder of this experience immediately before actual death, either by ourselves or by our master or our spiritual friends, so that we are ready for our last moment.

3. To recognize the three great visions when they arise in the *bardo*.

These three are linked together. If we have a thorough experience of the arising of visions through *tögel* practice during our lifetime, this enables us clearly to remember the practice and the nature of the visions the moment before death so that we can easily recognize them when they arise in the *bardo*. We can thereby obtain liberation in the clear light *bardo* by integrating in the base essence. This recognition is the principal reason we work with vision in *tögel* practice.

In the clear light *bardo* it is important for the average practitioner to remember his master, the teachings, and his practice. An inferior practitioner who has had no experience of dark retreat must try to understand that the visions that arise are his own manifestations, like a dream, and not be distracted by being attracted to or disturbed by them.

The Bardo of Existence

The third *bardo* is called "the *bardo* of existence." The explanation of this *bardo* has three parts:

1. How this *bardo* arises;
2. How to "cut" it to self-liberate in this *bardo*;
3. How one can be deluded in this *bardo* and fall back into illusion.

As to the manner in which this *bardo* arises: all the visions of deities, mandalas, and lights of the clear light *bardo* cease. Our mind is no longer supported by these visions and we begin to feel very frightened and think that we cannot change anything any more. The mind is without support. Our experience is as in a dream. We can move anywhere without anything stopping us. We have a mental image of our body but no physical body, and the only sense perception we have is mental. As soon as we think of a place, we arrive there. We think of doing many things but cannot actualize them. Our experience of our self is as in our previous life—we have the mental image of the mind—body we had when alive as well as all the tendencies to act and to get into circumstantial situations.

In order to cut through the experience of the existence *bardo* and obtain liberation, we must realize that our consciousness principle is in the *bardo*. For example, if we start to visit friends' and relatives' houses, we notice we are unable to communicate with them and that nobody answers or pays any attention to us when we call them. Nobody offers us a chair or a plate when we come to the dinner table. We may observe that our physical body in fact has been cremated. Rather than feeling disappointed at that moment when we notice such things or thinking that something is wrong, we should understand that we are dead and remember the teachings and our practice.

In the *bardo* of existence, it has become quite difficult to avoid being distracted and misguided by the visions. If we do not recognize them as expressions of the final view of emptiness, as a dream or as our own manifestation, in this *bardo* it is very easy to fall back into illusion. To prevent this, any practice will be helpful, especially if our Lama and spiritual friends practice for us.

Three Bardos and Three Levels of Practitioners

These three *bardos* correspond to the three levels or qualities of practitioners described earlier.

If we are a superior practitioner we obtain realization in the fundamental base *bardo* and do not go through the other *bardos* unless we consciously decide to return in the next life as a Nirmanakaya to help others. We integrate the single essence with presence and liberate the body, voice, and mind, opening them to enlightenment. In the Bon scriptures the superior practitioner is compared to the son of a lion or an eagle, or to the garuda that generates its own energy while in the egg after its mother has made a nest in space. The energies are various activities such as, for instance, flying, so that when the baby garuda hatches from the egg, it can immediately do everything the mother can do. The body is like the egg, and the mind is like the garuda: we are generating energy in our practice so that when we leave the body we are immediately liberated, like the garuda leaving the cracked egg. When the mind and body separate, the mind can do anything, so the superior practitioner liberates in the fundamental base *bardo* like meeting an old friend.

By doing *tögel* practice, especially the dark retreat and the practice of the peaceful and wrathful deities, to prepare for the visions that arise in the after death state, as an average practitioner we will be able to understand the sound and movement of energy as our own manifestations. When we see the rainbow lights, deities, mandalas, *tiglés*, and colors, we will not follow after them but recognize them as mental projections. In this way we will self-liberate in the clear light *bardo*.

The inferior practitioner obtains realization in the existence *bardo*. He is said to be like a poor boy who realizes he is a king and reclaims his kingdom. In this *bardo* we have experiences that make us think we are still alive and thereby create attachment to life, but if we understand that we are dead, it is like realizing our kingship, and the kingdom we get is liberation.

All the practices we do in our life are preparation for death and for these three *bardos*.

The *bardo* experiences are different for practitioners and for people with no exposure to the teachings, or who have heard the teachings but have never practiced them. In the case of nonpractitioners, the kinds of *bardo* visions that arise depend on whether their mental attitude tends towards virtue or vice. When the visions arise in the clear light *bardo*, people dominated by the main emotional poisons of anger, attachment, and ignorance have visions corresponding to the colors of the three passions: yellow for attachment, red (or white) for anger, and blue for ignorance. They experience red storms at the top of the head, and through the causes of the three basic emotional poisons are reborn in the three inferior dimensions, the realms of hell-beings, of tormented beings or pretas, and of animals. People whose main emotional poison was pride experience the color white and are reborn in the realm of the gods. Those whose foremost passion was jealousy experience green and are reborn in the realm of the titans or demigods.

People who have naturally calm and compassionate minds experience the five colors blended together and are reborn in a pure human dimension where it is possible to receive and practice teachings, and perhaps have the opportunity to choose the mandala of their rebirth.

Samsara and Nirvana

Conventional Bon and Buddhist philosophy says that there is no beginning of samsara but there is an end to samsara, namely, when we attain realization. According to Dzogchen there is no beginning to samsara as such, but there is a beginning to individual samsara. The beginning of samsara is caused by ignorance. If we are deluded in the clear light and the existence *bardos* and fail to recognize the true nature of the lights and visions we experience, then we fall back into samsara and take another physical body, not consciously, but through attraction to the colored light of our dominant passion. The beginning of an individual's samsara is that moment of distraction, of ignorance and misunderstanding, during the intermediate state between death and the next life. Whether we are able to have presence, in that moment or not determines whether we return to samsara or attain nirvana. Understanding the nature of the death process and of the lights and visions in the *bardo* gives rise to the process of nirvana and achievement of the light body.

Advice on Practicing for the Bardo

The *bardo* state is said to be like a dream because just as it is difficult in dreams to be aware that we are dreaming, in the *bardo* it is difficult to realize that we are in the *bardo*. If we do manage to realize it, it is difficult to remain in a state of stability as there is no support or base. We can be blown about and influenced by anything and if we do manage to have a little stability it is easy to be influenced by secondary causes.

If we have received and practiced *bardo* teachings, they can prove more useful than any other teachings. But what should we practice? It is necessary to understand well the experiences we will encounter at death so that we can understand the process of the dissolution of the elements as it occurs. In preparation for the *bardo* visions, it is useful to do *zhitro* practice during the day, and the dream and the natural light practices during the night so that we do not waste our time when we are sleeping. We must not only recognize that we are dreaming, but realize presence in the dream. Many people who don't follow teachings also recognize when they are dreaming, but in our practice what we must do is to remain present and eventually direct and control the dream ourselves. This important training can make the difference between having presence or being deluded, between realization or illusion in the intermediate state, between samsara and nirvana.

The *bardo* teachings contain the essence of all the teachings and of all the virtues. Because the mind's last moment is the most important, the teachings on how to work with that moment are vital. The most important thing we can do to prepare ourselves for death is to become familiar with the death process so that at the actual moment of death we will remember what we have to do. In this context it is also useful to gain knowledge and experience of the death process by helping others at the moment of death, not only fellow practitioners but also ordinary people.

People with a strong, stable mind may be able to have some understanding, even if they have not received teachings. For those who have knowledge of the teachings, understanding will depend on how simple and straightforward our approach is and how well we have understood the explanations.

In fact the *bardo* teachings enclose the essence of all the teachings and of all the virtues. As mind's last moment is the most important, the quality of these teachings is truly great.

Appendices

Appendix I

The First Cycle: The Nine Ways

The Southern Treasures

The following is based on a traditional presentation of the *Nine Ways* taken from *Gab 'grel*, written and concealed by the eighth-century Bon sage Dranpa Namkha and later discovered by the *terton* Bande Misum (Ban dhe Mi gsum).

1. *The Way of the Shen Practice of Prediction (Phya gshen theg pa)*. This Way is particularly suitable for the ordinary dualistic attitudes typical of humans, as the approach is that of protecting the three doors of existence (body, voice, and mind) from negativities, and the specific methods are concerned mainly with the diagnosis and ritual harmonization of energy imbalances in the individual and nature. The "view" of this Way is compared to a spy who observes the enemy from a hill and in this way remains in control. The methods used are divination (*mo*), astrological and geomantic calculations (*rtsis*), rituals (*gto*) and medical diagnosis (*dpyad*), and therapies (*sman*).

There are various ways of performing divinations. Most of the divinations are connected with deities, which means that the diviner must first realize the practice of the deity. One of the main divinations is called the Zhang Zhung *juthig* and is also used by Tibetan Buddhists of the Nyingmapa school. One of the most famous and most widespread manuals of this type of divination was written by the famous Nyingmapa scholar, Ju Mipham. It consists of using cords of eight threads made from hairs of different animals. These are tied in pairs and then thrown onto the ground in order to form knots (of which there are three hundred and sixty main kinds) used for predicting the future. The three hundred and sixty knots also represent the retinue of Zhang Zhung Meri, the "Fire Mountain (*me ri*) Deity" of Zhang Zhung.

In the case of medical diagnosis it is important to test for two possible causes of illness: physical disease (*nad*) and influences from negative energies (*gdon*). Disease is diagnosed through testing the pulse and the urine to determine the type of illness and the necessary medical treatment. Provocations by negative energy or energy imbalance are discovered through divination and astrology and treated through ritual practice.

2. *The Way of the Shen of the Manifest World* (or of *The Production of Visible Signs*) (*snang gshen theg pa*). This way contains rituals to deal with phenomenal appearances, viewed as either (positive) gods (*lha*) who help and protect or (negative) demons (*'dre*) that harm and disturb human life. The emphasis is on learning to communicate with these energies, invoking the gods and repelling the demons, and the master of this Way is said to be like a tradesman who, because of his abilities to communicate with other traders, is able to satisfy everyone. The main practices comprise the four *Gyer* Portals, the nine *sKad gcong* and the forty-two *gTang rag*. According to the *gZi brjid* (*The Glorious Biography of Tonpa Shenrab*) the traditional division of the "Portals" is fourfold:

a) "The Black Waters (*chab nag*)," "the river, the portal of exorcism (*sel*)" which contains methods of invocation of deities and exorcism of demons through the declaration of the origin myth (*smrang*). There are many different rituals to exorcize negativities and bring benefits, such as the "white ritual of the primordial existent deity (*Ye srid lha gzung dkar po*)," "the multi-colored ritual of the primordial power of the deity with weapons (*Ye dbang gnyan*)," "the black ritual of the deity of primordial conquest (*Ye 'dul dmag gzhung*)." These three deities are also subsumed under the deity of mind (*thugs ka'i lha*)." Another important series of rituals are the four rituals of the *sGra bla'i dpa' khrom*.

b) "The White Waters (*chab dkar*),"which contains methods for eliminating the menacing influences of nine demons and ten 'vampires' or evil spirits. In order to overcome their negative influences, these nine demons are dispatched through ransom rituals, while the ten evil spirits must be buried, performing special rituals which culminate in the erection of stupas over the burial sites.

c) "The Phan yul, The Portal of Ransom by Equal Exchange," which comprises ritual methods of preparing substitute effigies or ransoms for victims (men, women, and children) to present to hostile spirits. The principle of this practice is to remove all negative karmic traces by paying off "karmic debts" incurred with other types of beings.

d) The "Master Guide (dPon gsas)," "The Portal of Rituals" for various nature spirits. This comprises various *sadhanas* (spiritual practices) addressed to deities (*lha gsas*) of different dimensions, such as the pantheon of wrathful deities of space (*bying gyi lha tshogs*), to male and female deities, to the Protectors, the Lords of the soil, and the *nagas*.

3. *The Way of the Shen of Magic Power* (*'phrul gshen theg pa*), which contains magic rituals for securing the help of nature in agriculture and also for disposing of enemies. This Way emphasizes the three principle activities of veneration, conjuration, and application (*bsnyan sgrub las*). The practitioner venerates his divine spiritual master, his parents, friends, and spiritual brothers and sisters, and values his own heart and eyes. The conjuration consists in going to a suitable place and there preparing the altar, the mandala, and the offering cakes. The application consists in the practices of visualization, mantra recitation, mudras, and invocation for enactment of the wrathful magic action. Finally, there is the concluding *sadhana*. The wrathful magic action of suppressing, burning, and repelling demons, evil and deceitful spirits that harm beings and the teachings is found in three divisions of Tantras: external (comprised in the maternal Tantras), internal (the paternal Tantras), and secret (in which the *bindus* of action, *las kyi thig le*) are applied.

4. *The Way of the Shen of Existence* (*srid gshen theg pa*). This is concerned mainly with the three hundred and sixty funerary and

propitiatory consecration rites (*dur*) and astrological calculations for the deceased in the intermediate (*bar do*) state. The intention is to guide the dead through the after-death state and protect them from disturbances by evil spirits. This way contains a classification of eighty-one causes of death: twenty by illnesses derived from severe heat or cold; twenty by accidents caused by negative energies and obstacles (*gdon gegs*); twenty by war weapons; twenty by secondary causes of the elements; only one is a karmic death by natural cause on the completion of a full life. This Way also contains ritual methods to ensure good health, good fortune, and long life for the living.

5. *The Way of the Virtuous Lay Practitioners* (*dge bsnyen theg pa*). This, the first of the four "fruit" vehicles, specifies ethical and moral rules (such as the ten virtues, the Ten Perfections, and the building of stupas) for laypersons.

6. *The Way of the Ascetic Sages* (*drang srong theg pa*). This lays down the strict ascetic disciplinary rules to be obeyed by fully ordained monks and nuns.

7. *The Way of the White A* (*a dkar theg pa*). This is concerned with the Tantric practice of transformation through visualization of oneself as the deity and the practices involving the mandala. Great power is accrued through these practices.

8. *The Way of Primordial Shen* (*ye gshen theg pa*) is concerned with esoteric tantric practices. It describes in detail the relationship with the Tantric master, consort practice, the generation (*bskyed rim*) and accomplishment (*rdzogs rim*) phases of Tantric practice of transformation into the personal sacred deity (*yi dam*), and the highly unconventional behavior of the perfected "crazy wisdom" sage.

9. *The Supreme Way* (*bla med theg pa*) describes the absolute base (*kun gzhi*) of enlightenment and illusion, the path (*lam*), the mind abiding in its primordial natural state, and the fruit (*bras bu*), enlightenment and the supreme attainments. The ninth Way comprises the teachings of Dzogchen, the "Great Perfection." It expounds the view, meditation, and application of the direct and immediate Dzogchen path and describes the accomplishment of Dzogchen, realization of enlightenment in one's very lifetime.

The Central Treasures

The Nine Ways of the Central Treasures are divided into the Ways of Cause and Ways of the Fruit.

The lower Ways of cause are:

1. *The Way of Gods and Men where One Relies upon Another (Lha mi gzhan rten gyi theg pa).*

2. *The Way of Those Who Understand by Themselves and Who Follow Shenrab (Rang rtogs gshen rab kyi theg pa).*

The higher Ways of cause are:

3. *The Way of the Compassionate Bodhisattvas (Thugs rje sems pa'i theg pa).* In this Way it is necessary to understand the inherent lack of independent existence of the self and of phenomena, to practice the Ten *Paramita* (generosity, morality, patience, diligence, meditation, strength, compassion, commitment, skillful means, and wisdom). Thereby one attains the perfect Buddhahood of the Trikaya.

4. *The Way of the Bodhisattvas which is without Conceptual Elaboration (gYung drung sems dpa'spros med pa'i theg pa).* In this Way it is necessary to understand the impermanent and empty nature of the self and of phenomena, to practice the Ten Paramita and the Four Collections (generosity, friendly speech, practicing according to the meaning, and teaching in harmony with the meaning according to the intellectual capacity of the students). Thereby one attains the perfect Buddhahood of the Trikaya.

The outer Tantric paths:

5. *The Way of the Primordial Bon of Pure Conduct and Ritual Activity (Bya ba gtsang spyod ye bon gyi theg pa).* This is the Way of Kriyatantra and emphasizes pure conduct. It is necessary to establish oneself in the original condition of the natural state without modification, worship the "knowledge being" (*ye shes pa*) as a Lord, and practice the Ten Paramitas and Four Collections. Thereby one attains the perfect Buddhahood of the Trikaya.

6. *The Way of the Clear Knowledge Which Knows All Aspects* (*rNam pa kun ldan mngon shes kyi theg pa*). This is the Way of Charyatantra. It is necessary to establish oneself in the original condition of the natural state without modification, honor the "knowledge being" as a brother, and practice the Ten Paramitas and four collections. Thereby one attains the perfect Buddhahood of the Trikaya.

The inner Tantric paths:

7. *The Way of the Manifestation of Compassion as Actual Visualization* (*dNgos bskyed thugs rje rol pa'i theg pa*). In this Way it is necessary to establish oneself in the higher view of the absolute truth, remaining in the original condition of the natural state without modification and practicing the visualization process of generation (*bskyed rim*) of the transformation deity. Thereby one attains the perfect Buddhahood of the Trikaya.

8. *The Way Wherein Everything is Perfect and Meaningful* (*Shin tu don ldan kun rdzogs kyi theg pa*). In this Way it is necessary to establish oneself in the higher view of the absolute truth, remaining without modification in the original condition of the natural state where space and awareness are inseparable and to practice the visualization process of perfection (*rdzogs rim*) of the transformation deity. Thereby one attains the perfect Buddhahood of the Trikaya.

9. *The Unsurpassed Way of the Highest Summit of Primordial Dzogchen* (*Ye nas rdzogs chen yang rtse bla med kyi theg pa*). This Way comprises three series of teachings: Semde (*sems sde*), the series of teachings on the mind and on the essential emptiness of the natural state; Longde (*klong sde*), the series of teachings on space and on the natural clarity of the natural state; and Menagde (*man ngag sde*), the series of secret instructions on the inseparability of emptiness and clarity manifesting as compassionate energy (*thugs rje*). In the Menagde the path consists in the practice of *trekchö* and *tögel*, whereby one attains the perfect Buddhahood of the Trikaya and achieves the *jalu* (*'ja' lus*), the rainbow or light body.

Appendix II

The Second Cycle: Four Portals and the Fifth, the Treasury

The Four Portals and the Fifth, the Treasury, are:

1. *The Bon of White Water of Wrathful Mantras* (*Chab dkar drag po snags kyi bon*), consisting in esoteric Tantric practices involving recitation of wrathful mantras: the "nine base entrances" (*bsnyen pa'i gzhi ma sgo dgu*), the "eighteen branches of *sadhanas*" (*bsgrub pa'i yan lag bco brgyad*) and the "nine actions of the great Chong" (*mChong chen sde dgu*). These nine actions are: rites of prognostication using a mirror (*gsal byed me long pra yi 'phyong*); rites of propitiation of various deities (*mkha' klong rab 'byams bskong ba'i 'phyong*); funerary rites (*nyi zer zhags pa 'dur gyi 'phyong*); rites of cursing ('*od zer 'khyil pa sman gyi 'phyong*); rites using fire (*las bzhi rgyun lnga sbyin sreg 'phyong*); rites of the renewal of faith ('*gu ya srog 'dzin dbang gi 'phyong*); meditative wisdom practices (*ye shes rtse rgyal lta ba'i 'phyong*); higher esoteric practices (*thig le dgu pa nyams 'phyong*). They belong to the Chipung (*sPyi spungs*) cycle of teachings.

2. *The Bon of Black Water of Tantras of Existence* (*Chab nag srid pa rgyud kyi bon*), consisting in various rituals (magical, prognosticatory and divinatory, funerary, for ransoms, etc.) for purification.

3. *The Bon of the Hundred Thousand Verse Sutra of the Land of Phan* (*'Phan yul rgyas pa 'bum gyi bon*), consisting in rules for monks and laymen, with philosophical explanations.

4. *The Bon of the Oral Guidance and Secret Instructions of the Master Sage* (*dPon gsas man ngag lung gyi bon*), consisting in teachings and precepts for Dzogchen practices.

5. *The Bon of the Treasury, which is Highest and All-Embracing* (*gTsang mtho thog spyi rgyug mdzod kyi bon*), comprises the essential aspects of all four portals.

Appendix III

Concerning the Zhang Zhung Nyan Gyud

The *Zhang Zhung Nyan Gyud* is now a vast collection of texts, comprising over 700 pages of root Tantras of teachings, volumes of commentaries and collections of experiences of the lineage masters used as guides for practice. There are also sections on the early history of Zhang Zhung and Tibet.

To give an example of these teachings, let us examine the *Instructions on the Six Lights* (*sGron ma drug gi gdams pa*). The first light (or chapter), *gNas pa gzhi'i sgron ma ngo bo ji lta gnas pa kun gzhi ngos 'dzin gnad*, "the method for recognizing the base of all (*kun gzhi*), the essence of the original nature of existence," explains that the true nature of the base of phenomenal existence is emptiness. The second chapter, *Tsi ta sha'i sgron ma gzhi gang na gnas pa rang rig klong shar gyi gnad*, "the method that illustrates how the light of original wisdom shines within the physical heart," explains that the light of original wisdom abides within the human heart of flesh and blood. The third chapter, *dKar 'jam rtsa'i sgron ma lam gang las pyung pa ye shes zang thal gyi gnad*, "the method that illustrates how the unhindered wisdom arises in the path of light of the white central channel," explains the subtle channels of the yogic body in which the light of wisdom circulates without obstruction. The fourth chapter, *rGyang zhags chu'i sgron ma sgo gang la shar ba rig pa gcer mthong gi gnad*, "the method that illustrates how naked vision of original wisdom arises through the light-water doors (i.e. the eyes)," explains the methods of contemplation of original wisdom which undifferentiatedly pervades inner and outer reality alike. All phenomenal existence is explained as being a projection of the original light that resides in the physical heart and manifests through the eyes; this implies that objective concrete reality is merely illusion. The fifth chapter, *Zhing khams sprod kyi sgron ma lam ci ltar nyams su blang pa sku gsum dmar thag bcad pa'i gnad*, "the method that illustrates the irrevocable decision to undertake the Trikaya practice through the light that introduces the pure dimensions," explains the initiatory contemplation practices whereby the pure dimensions manifest to the Dzogchenpa through rays of rainbow light and sounds. The sixth chapter, *Bar do dus kyi sgron ma 'khrul rtogs kyi so tshams gang la thug pa 'kor 'das gyes tshul gyi gnad ston pa,* "the teaching on the method of the light in the bardo, where one reaches the limits of illusion and understanding, the separation of samsara and nirvana," explains the practices to perform in the after-death bardo state where understanding reality leads to liberation and illusion to return to samsara.

The Lineage Masters of the Zhang Zhung Nyan Gyud

Spiritual teachings do not spring from the thought consciousness of the human founders of religions in physical space-time but awaken in their deep consciousness and are ultimately derived from the "space of religion" beyond chronological time and geographical place.

The long transmission of the Dzogchen teachings of the *Zhang Zhung Nyan Gyud* Bon tradition are derived from the *bon ku* (*bon sku*), the "essence body or dimension" of reality that is the *kunzhi* (*kun gzhi*) base of the great perfection. In the great unconditioned realm beyond space, which is primordially pure (*ka dag*), beyond samsara and nirvana and spontaneously perfected (*lhun sgrub*) with all the potential qualities, where there is no cause, no external dimension (universe) or internal dimension (beings contained in the universe), no form and no color, lies the "paradise of space," the citadel where the primordial master (*ye nyid ston pa*) Self-Arising Awareness, the *bon ku* (*dharmakaya*; cf. *chos sku*, the truth body in Buddhism) Buddha Kuntuzangpo (Kun tu bZang po, Skt. Samantabhadra) gave the teachings to the "perfection body" (*rDzogs sku*: *Sambhogakaya*; cf. *klong sku*, the enjoyment body in Buddhism) Buddha Shenlha Okar (gShen lha 'Od dkar) by direct mind transmission. Without concepts or words, Samantabhadra mentally transmitted the four series of teachings of Bon Dzogchen:

1. *Phyi lta ba spyi spyod*, "the outer general view"; these are the introductory teachings.

2. *Nang man ngag dmar khrid*, "the inner direct essential instruction."

3. *gSang ba rig pa gcher mthong*, "the secret *rigpa* naked awareness"; these are secret teachings on methods of meditation on light.

4. *Yang gsang gnas lugs phug chod,* "the discovery of the innermost secret natural state of being"; these are the most esoteric teachings.

Shenlha Okar, in his turn, transmitted the teachings to his "mind and thought" disciple the "manifestation body" (*sprul sku*) Tonpa Shenrab Miwoche, who in his turn transmitted the teachings in this world dimension in Zhang Zhung by mind transmission without words (*dgongs brgyud*).

Thus these teachings were gradually handed down in this way by the lineage of nine masters of the mind transmission (*dgongs rgyud dgu*) from Zhang Zhung:

1. Ye nid kyi ston pa Kuntuzangpo
2. Thugs rje'i ston pa Shenlha Okar
3. sPrul pa'i ston pa Shenrab Miwo
4. Tseme Oden (Tshan med 'od ldan)
5. Tulshen Nangden ('Phrul gshen snang ldan)
6. Barnang Khujuk (Bar snang khu byug)
7. Yum Zangza Ringzun (Yum bzang za ring tsun)
8. Chimed Tsugphu ('Chi med gtsug phud)
9. Sangwa Dupa (gSang ba 'dus pa)

The mind transmission lineage was followed by the lineage of twenty-four great masters (*gang zag nyi bzhi*) of the Zhang Zhung Nyan Gyud, "the oral transmission of Zhang Zhung," so called because all twenty-four masters were from Zhang Zhung and used speech to transmit the teachings.

1. gShen Hor ti Chen po
2. Kun mkhyen Don sgrub
3. Tshe spung Zla ba rGyal mtshan
4. Ra sangs Klu rgyal
5. Ta pi ra tsa
6. Ra sangs Ku ma ra tsa
7. Ra sangs bSam grub
8. Zhang Zhung Sad ne ha'u
9. Gu rib Lha sbyin
10. Gu rib dPal bzang
11. Ra sangs Khrin ne khod

12. Jag rong gSas mkhar

13. Khyung po A ba ldong

14. Khyung po bKra sis rGyal mtshan

15. Khyung po Legs mgon

16. Ma hor sTag gzig

17. Don grub Legs pa Klu'i sras

18. Zhang Zhung Khra sna sTag sgro

19. Zhang Zhung 'Yu lo

20. Zhang Zhung Khri pa

21. Khyung po Legs mgon

22. Ma hor sTag gzig

23. Gu rib Sin slag can

24. (Gyer spungs) sNang bzher Lod po

These illustrious masters of the Bon tradition, who all attained the rainbow body, foimed an uninterrupted lineage of transmission from master to disciple, known at that time as the "single transmission" (*gcig rgyud*) from the master to one single disciple. In fact the transmission was often given through a hollow reed or bamboo pipe, directly from the master's mouth into the disciple's ear, so that it could not be spread by the wind and heard by anyone else. The master who had experienced the truth of the teaching found the right disciple to whom to hand on all his knowledge through the transmission of his living experience, and only after the master's death did the disciple start to transmit the teaching in his own turn. However, it was not always easy to find the right disciple to whom to transmit the teaching, as we will see below in the example of Tapihritsa. Before Tapihritsa, the lineage masters entrusted the teachings to one single disciple to continue the transmission; Tapihritsa told his own disciples that it was all right to teach more than one person, even two or three hundred people, but first the master must ascertain whether the disciples are suitable to receive the teachings.

Each of these twenty-four masters experienced the results of the practice in different ways and left a transmission of teachings, explanations, and meditation methods based on their own personal experiences (*nyams rgyud*) to their disciples; in the eleventh century these were put in writing and collected. I received these teachings during a twenty-four day retreat; each day we practiced according to the experiential explanation of one of the masters, visualizing him in the form of the guru yoga deity Shenlha Okar (who symbolizes the union of all the lineage masters) so that his personal experience could penetrate deeply into us.

The main practice of all these masters was Dzogchen contemplation, and as support of the fundamental practice, they performed the practices of the tutelary deities Meri and Gekhod, the principal divinities of Zhang Zhung. Zhang Zhung Meri is associated with Mount Kailash and is very closely tied to the transmission of the *Zhang Zhung Nyan Gyud* teachings.

Glossary of Names

All-Victorious Ones of Space — *Kun dbying rgyal ba'i dkyil 'khor*

black ritual of the diety of primordial conquest — *Ye 'dul dmag gzhung*

Black Waters — *Chab nag*

Bon of Black Water of Tantras of Existence — *Chab nag srid pa rgyud kyi bon*

Bon of the Hundred Thousand Verse Sutra of the Land of Phan — *'Phan yul rgyas pa 'bum gyi bon*

Bon of the Oral Guidance and Secret Instructions of the Master Sage — *dPon gsas man ngag lung gyi bon*

Bon of the Treasury Which Is Highest and All-Embracing — *gTsang mtho thog spyi rgyug mdzod kyi bon*

Bon of White Water of Wrathful Mantras — *Chab dkar drag po sngags kyi bon*

Bonpo Master — *Lopon Tenzin Namdak Rinpoche*

Bonpo Master — *Lopon Sangye Tenzin Rinpoche*

Bonpo Master Shardza Rinpoche — *Shar rdza bkra shis rgyal mtshan*

Buddha Shenlha okar — *gShen lha 'Od dkar*

Continent of the Hundred Thousand Gesars that is the Castle of the Lha — *gSas Khang Ge sar 'Bum gling*

Dampa Togkar — *Dam pa tog dkar*

deity connected with the blue light — *dGa' ba Don grup*

deity connected with the green light — *dGe lha Gar phyug*

deity connected with the red light — *Che drag Ngos med*

deity connected with the white light — *Kun snang Khyab pa*

deity connected with the yellow light	*gSal wa Rang byung*
deity of mind	*thugs kyi lha*
fire mountain deity	*Zhang Zhung Meri*
Five Ways of Fruit	*'Bras bu'i theg pa lnga*
Four Bon Portals and the Fifth, the Treasury	*Bon sgo bzhi mdzod lnga*
Four Ways of Cause	*rGyu'i theg pa bzhi*
funerary deities	*Mkha' klong rab 'byams bskong ba*
Bon text of Dzogchen logic	*Gal mdo*
Glorioug biography of Tonpa Shenrab	*'Dus pa rin po che'i rgyud dri ma pa gzi brjid rab tu 'bar ba'i mdo*
Great Expanse of the Zenith of Dzogchen	*Bla med rDzogs chen yang rtse klong chen*
Indestructible Peak that is the Castle of the Lha	*Sas Khang gYung drung Lha tse*
Instructions on the Six Lights	*sGron ma drug gi gdams pa*
Khyabpa Lagring	*Khyab pa lag ring*
King Trisong Detsen	*Khri srong lde'u btsan*
Ladag Nagdro	*Lha dag sNgag dro*
mandala of the Pure Lotus Mother	*rNam dag Pad ma Yum chen gyi dkyil 'khor*
Master Guide to the Portal of Rituals	*dPon gsas*
Mirror of the Luminous Mind	*'Od gsal sems kyi me long*
Mount Kailash	*Gangs chen Ti se*
Mucho Demdrug	*Mu cho lDem drug*
Nagas	*klu*
name of text	*'Brig mtshams mtha' dkar*
name of text	*'Dus pa rin po che'i rgyud gzer mig*
name of text	*bsGrags pa sKor gsum*
nine actions of the great Chong	*mChong chen sde dgu*
Nine Ways of Bon	*Theg pa rim dgu'i bon*
Nine Ways of Everlasting Bon	*gYung drung bon theg pa rim dgu*
Nyamed Sherab Gyaltsen	*mNyam med Shes rab rGyal mtshan*
oral transmission from the country of Zhang-Zhung	*Zhang Zhung Nyan Gyud*
Rasang Lugyal	*Ra sangs klu rgyal*
Silver Palace of the Garuda Valley	*Khyung lung dngul mkhar*
Tapihritsa	*Ta pi hri tsa*
teacher of Tapihritsa	*(Gyer spungs) sNang bzher Lod po*
Union of the Four Chakras	*'Kor lo bzhi sbrags*
Unsurpassed Way of the Highest Summit of Primordial Dzogchen	*Ye nas rdzogs chen yang rtse bla med kyi theg pa*
Way of Compassionate Bodhisattvas	*Thugs rje sems pa'i theg pa*

Way of Gods and Men where One Relies upon Another	*Lha mi gzhan rten gyi theg pa*
Way of Primordial Shen	*Ye gshen theg pa*
Way of the Ascetic Sages	*Drang srong theg pa*
Way of the Bodhisattvas Which is Without Conceptual Elaboration	*gYung drung sems dpa' spros med pa'i theg pa*
Way of the clear knowledge which knows all aspects	*rNam pa kun ldan mngon shes kyi theg pa*
Way of the Manifestation of Compassion as Actual Visualization	*dNgos bskyed thugs rje rol pa'i theg pa*
Way of the Primordial Bon of Pure Conduct and Ritual Activity	*Bya ba gtsang spyod ye bon gyi theg pa*
Way of the Shen of Existence	*Srid gshen theg pa*
Way of the Shen of Magic Power	*'Phrul gshen theg pa*
Way of the Shen of the Manifest World	*sNang gshen theg pa*
Way of the Shen Practice of Prediction	*Phya gshen theg pa*
Way of the Virtuous Lay Practitioners	*dGe bsnyen theg pa*
Way of the White A	*A dkar theg pa*
Way of Those who Understand by themselves and who follow Shenrab	*Rang rtogs gshen rab kyi theg pa*
Way wherein Everything is Perfect and Meaningful	*Shin tu don ldan kun rdzogs kyi theg pa*
White ritual of the primordial existent deity	*Ye srid lha gzung dkar po*
White Waters	*Chab dkar*
Yungdrung ling Monastery	*gYung drung gling*

Glossary of Terms

absolute reality	*gnas lug mthar thug*
accomplishment phase	*rdzogs rim*
agitation	*rgod pa*
animals	*byol song*
application	*las*
arrow way	*mda' lam*
astrological and geomantic calculations	*rtsis*
awakened awareness	*rig pa*
bindus of action	*las kyi thig le*
base	*kun gzhi*
being without top or bottom	*kha gting med pa*
body of light	*'ja' lus pa*
body of perfection	*rdzogs sku*
boundlessness	*mu med pa*
calm abiding in tranquiflity	*zhi gnas*
clarity	*gsal ba*
clear light	*'od gsal*
conjuration	*sgrub*
contemplative equipoise	*mnyam bzhag*
conventional conceptual analytic mind	*tha snyad tshad ma lhan bcas*
dark retreat	*mun tshams*
deluded mind	*ma rig pa*
demigods	*lha ma yin*
demons	*'dre*
devas	*lha*
dharma	*chos*
dialectics school	*bshad 'dra*
discovery of the innermost secret natural state of being	*yang gsang gnas lugs phug chod*
disease	*mod*

divination	*mo*
eighteen branches of sadhanas	*bsgrub pa'i yan lag bco brgyad*
emptiness	*stong pa*
energy	*rtsal*
energy of clear light	*'od gsal gyi snang ba*
essence	*ngo bo*
essence body	*bon sku*
essential nature	*ngo bo nyid*
everlastingness	*zad pa med pa*
exhaustion of phenomena	*bon nyid zad pa*
experience	*nyams*
experience of bliss	*bde ba'i nyams*
experience of clarity	*gsal ba'i nyams*
experience of emptiness	*stong pa'i nyams*
external	*snang ldan*
external space	*mkha'*
external arising of awareness	*rang rig khong shar*
five pure lights, the	*öd-nga*
fixation with an attribute	*mtshan bchas*
fixation without an attribute	*mtshan med*
forced introduction of the clear light	*'od gsal btsan thabs su ngo sprad*
four visions	*snang bzhi*
fruit	*bras bu*
generation phase	*bskyed rim*
gods	*lha*
grasping the mind	*sems 'dzin*
great vastness	*bdal pa chen po*
guide instructions for the intermediate state	*bar do thos grol*
guide of A	*A-khrid*
higher esoteric practices	*thig le dgu pa nyams kyi 'phyong*
hitting a nail	*gzer bu*
human beings	*mi*
immutability	*'gyur ba med pa*
increasing vision	*nyams snang gong 'phel*
inherent self-light of awareness	*rig pa'i rang 'od*
inherent self-rays of awareness	*rig pa'i rang zer*
inherent self-sound of awareness	*rig pa'i rang sgra*
inner direct essential instruction	*man ngag ngang dmar khrid*
inner mental space	*nang dbying*
inner precepts	*nang gsum*
inseparability of clarity and emptiness	*gsal stong gnyis med*
insight meditation	*lhag mthong*
integration	*nyams len bsre ba*
internal space	*klong*

no more training	*mi slob lam*
non-grasping mind	*'dzin pa med pa'i sems*
omnipervasive wisdom	*ye shes spyi blugs*
omnipervasiveness	*'byams yas pa*
one life and one body	*tse gcig lus gcig*
one taste	*ro gcig*
one's own direct experience	*nyams su myang*
oral tradition	*bka' ma*
ordinary attainments	*thun mong gi dngos grub*
outer general view	*phyi lta ba spyi spyod*
outer precepts	*phyi gsum*
path	*lam*
path of accumulation	*tsogs lam*
path of preparation	*sbyor lam*
path of renunciation	*spang lam*
person	*gang zag*
personal sacred deity	*yi dam*
pervading awareness	*chab rig*
physical matter	*rdul phran*
postmeditation	*rje thob*
portal of exorism	*sel*
Portal of Ransom by Equal Exchange	*'phan yul*
processing agreement	*bzhed ldan*
practice session	*thun*
presence	*dran rig*
pretas	*yi dags*
primordial awareness	*ye rig*
primordial Buddha	*Kun tu zang po*
primordially pure	*ka dag*
radiance	*gdangs*
rays	*zer*
ripening of vision	*rig pa tshad 'phebs*
rites of cursing	*'od ser 'khyil pa sman gyi 'phyong*
rites of prognostication using a mirror	*gsal byed me long pra yi 'phyong*
rites of renewal of faith	*'gu ya srog 'dzin dbang gi 'phyong*
rites of using fire	*las bzhi rgyun lnga sbyin sreg 'phyong*
rituals	*gto*
secret gaze	*gsang ba 'gying ba'i lta stangs*
secret instruction series	*man ngag sde*
secret space	*dbying*
seeds of light	*thig le*
self	*nga*
self-arising Awareness	*ye nyid ston pa*
self-arising self-liberation	*rang shar rang grol*

self-clarity	*rang gsal*
self-knowing	*rang rig*
self-liberation	*grol lam*
self-liberation on arising	*gcer lta gcer grol*
self-originated wisdom	*rang 'byung ye shes*
self-possessing	*rang ldan*
self-understanding wisdom	*rang rig ye shes*
sign	*rtags*
signs of spiritual progress	*zin rtags*
single great sphere	*thig le chen po*
single pointed contemplation	*mkhregs chod*
single sphere of totality	*thig le nyag cig*
sky gazing	*rig pa nam mkhar gtad*
son	*bu*
soul	*bla*
sound	*sgra*
space series	*klong sde*
spiritual mind treasure	*dgongs gter*
spontaneously perfected	*lhun sgrub*
stable tranquillity	*thar thug gi zhi gnas*
startled awareness	*he de wa*
supreme attainments	*mchog gi dngos grub*
supreme way	*bla med theg pa*
third path of seeing	*mthong lam*
thought	*rtog pa*
three dimensions, the	*sku gsum*
transparent nakedness	*zang thal gcer bu*
uncontractedness	*dog pa med pa*
unlimited expansiveness	*yongs su rgya ma chad pa*
unmeasurableness	*dpag tu med pa*
unobscured self-clarity	*me long sgrib med rang gsal*
unobstructed compassion	*ma 'gag pa*
veneration	*bsnyan*
view	*lta ba*
visible support	*dmigs rten*
wheel gaze	*khor lo 'gying ba'i lta stangs*
wheel of realization and illusion	*rtogs khrul rten 'brel gi 'khor lo*
wheel of the intermediate state	*bar do dus kyi 'khor lo*
wheel of the points of the body	*lus gnad rtsa'i 'khor lo*
wheel of the primordial base	*gnas pa gzhi 'khor lo*
working with light	*rthod rgal*
wrathful deities of space	*dbying gyi lha tshogs*
yogi	*rnal 'byor pa*

Sources of Quotations at Beginnings of Chapters

The Ligmincha Institute

may be reached at

P.O. Box 1892
Charlottesville, VA 22903 U.S.A.
Tel: (804) 977-6161
Fax: (804) 977-7020
e-mail: Ligmincha@aol.com